From Jute to Jungle

Also by Carol Purves:

Chinese Whispers
        One Day Publications   1 903087 57 0

From Prussia with Love
        One Day Publications   184625008 0

Travels with Frances Ridley Havergal
        One Day Publications   978 1 846625 206 8

Amazonian Missionary
        Obtainable as a Kindle book.

From Jute to Jungle

The Mary Slessor Story

Carol Purves

DB
DIADEM BOOKS

From Jute to Jungle:
The Mary Slessor Story
All Rights Reserved. Copyright © 2014 **Carol Purves**

No part of this book may be reproduced or transmitted in any form or by any means, graphic, electronic, or mechanical, including photocopying, recording, taping or by any information storage or retrieval system, without the permission in writing from the copyright holder.

The right of Carol Purves to be identified as the author of this work has been asserted in accordance with the Copyright, Designs and Patents Act 1988 sections 77 and 78.

The views expressed in this work are solely those of the author and do not necessarily reflect the views of the publisher, and the publisher hereby disclaims any responsibility for them.

Photo of stained glass window thanks to the McManus Museum in Dundee.

Published by Diadem Books
For information, please contact:

Diadem Books
16 Lethen View
Tullibody
Scotland
FK10 2GE

www.diadembooks.com

ISBN: 978-1-291-75378-3

Acknowledgements

I wish to express my sincere thanks for the help I received in the writing of this work from Colin, Barbara and Philip, Sue and Rob, Libby and Michael and Kathleen.

'It is by grace you have been saved—through faith and this is not from yourselves; it is the gift of God.'
(Ephesians 2:8.)

'The world and its desires pass away, but the man who does the will of God lives for ever.'
(1 John 2:17.)

TABLE OF CONTENTS

Introduction		1
Chapter 1	A Wee Scottish Lassie	3
Chapter 2	Missionaries for Africa	13
Chapter 3	God's Choice of Continent	24
Chapter 4	Family and Furloughs	34
Chapter 5	Twin Tragedies	44
Chapter 6	Into the Jungle	51
Chapter 7	Successes and Superstitions	61
Chapter 8	Friends and Failures	71
Chapter 9	Mary's Secret Weapon	80
Chapter 10	Letters from Africa	85
Chapter 11	The Honoured Missionary	89
Chapter 12	The Work Completed	97
Chapter 13	The Work Goes On	105
Bibliography		110
Review by Irene Howat		111

INTRODUCTION

MARY SLESSOR was born in Aberdeen in 1848, the second child of a Christian mother and drunken father. Before Robert Slessor died prematurely the family moved to a slum in Dundee where Mary commenced work in a jute factory.

Having had her sinful ways pointed out to her she gave her life to Christ and commenced working among the slum children in the city. She felt called to become a missionary in Calabar in Nigeria. After training in Edinburgh she sailed to Africa where many cultural shocks awaited her.

Her biggest campaign was against the practice of killing twin babies. Her life was often in danger from the natives, the treacherous wildlife and her own failing health. Gradually conditions improved and the life of women in Africa became easier.

As she penetrated deeper and deeper into the jungle Mary was best when working on her own. Because she lived as a native the Africans accepted her when they didn't always accept the oppressive British presence.

In all she had five furloughs back in Scotland where she tried to recruit other workers, but eventually her health failed and she had to resort to being wheeled around in a cart. Throughout her life she worked tirelessly for her Master.

Mary died at the age of sixty-six in 1915, having been presented with the Order of the Hospital of St John of Jerusalem as well as being a Consul in the Native Court.

Simply buried with just a cross to mark her grave, she was nevertheless remembered in her native Dundee by a magnificent stained glass window in the city museum, plus a special corner devoted entirely to her life and work. Scotland further honoured her by placing her image on their bank notes. A number of plays are still being performed about her life as well as poems written in her honour.

Chapter 1

A WEE SCOTTISH LASSIE

'**WE'LL DO FOR YOU**, if you don't leave us alone!'
'I'll not give up on you. You can do what you like to me.' The feisty Mary Slessor had an answer for the dark-haired, wiry street lad from Dundee who was taunting her.

She stood her ground as out of his pocket he produced a lump of lead tied to a length of string and swung it round and round her head. Mary had seen this kind of weapon before but this was the first time she'd been threatened with it.

'I'll strike a deal with you. If you swing that lead as near me as you can and I don't flinch, you must promise to come to the mission with me and then when in there you must behave.'

The urchin smirked. He knew she would soon flinch; she was only a girl anyway.

The bullying lad gradually swung the lead nearer and nearer, the draught of the weight disturbing her ginger ringlets and at one point slightly grazing her forehead. She couldn't check if it was bleeding as she never moved though she was definitely quaking inside. Eventually he gave up; he knew when he was beaten.

'We can't force her boys, she's game.'

'I've not backed down,' she said. 'Now you can't back down on me. Come into the mission.'

Every week the street lad had seen Mary walking purposefully into the Wishart Church hall in one of the poorer parts of Dundee. They knew she was attending some sort of

'Christian' meeting and they thought they could frighten her away but they hadn't reckoned on her grit and determination. Now Mary had turned the tables on them. There was no choice but to reluctantly follow her into the hall.

Years later Mary had on display in her African hut a photo of this same young lad, his wife and family. That day in Dundee was a turning point in his life. He started to abandon his wild ways and eventually learn to love the Lord. The photo was one of the few possessions that Mary still had in her hut when she died.

The origin of the surname Slessor is obscure, though it is thought to be Anglo-Scottish. In a time when spelling was more random variations included Slassor and Sletar.

Mary had begun her life further north. The icy blasts from the North Pole had lost little of their severity before they hit the shores of this city of Aberdeen on the rugged east coast of Scotland. Born at Oldmeldrum, probably in 1822, Mary's mother Mrs Slessor, had been christened Mary Mitchell and was the only child from a well-to-do home. She had married Robert Slessor, born in Buchan probably in 1816, who was now a local shoemaker. She knew he liked a drink but thought that with her Christian influence he would be able to break the habit. She wasn't to know that whenever he faced hardship and tragedy he would only spend more time and money drowning his sorrows.

On 2nd December 1848 their second child was born at Mutton Brae in Aberdeen, a little girl, Mary. No-one knew then that this little mite born in the cold climes of Scotland would die sixty-six years later in the steaming jungle of the Calabar region of Africa. The intervening years would be packed with adventure, danger and illness in an era when on the whole women did not stray far from the confines of their family. Because of her life and work the name of Mary Slessor is still remembered and revered today.

There was only one reason for this life becoming remarkable. It was Mary's love of God and her devotion to His will for her life. Her change of continent was not a need to escape the harsh realities of Scotland, nor was it solely a love of coloured babies, though because of her love of God, she did love them. It was only the love of God which upheld her through physical danger, hardship, loneliness and heart-ache. Duty can call missionaries but only love can keep them there; the love of God.

The cold bleak city of Aberdeen housed numerous factories; establishments which provided employment and pollution. The poverty of Mary's family was typical of so many. As a shoemaker Mary's father toiled twelve hours a day, his hands blackened by the continual working with leather and his teeth damaged with gritting on brads for his trade. Mary watched him working, fascinated as a stream of customers came into his shop, for even at a young age she was interested in people. But she was also acutely aware that some of their neighbours never visited her father. Such was their poverty that they had no shoes which needed to be mended. In Aberdeen barefooted children were a common sight.

Bob, an easy-going, slightly balding man, lived for Saturdays which was payday. This was his time of glory.

'Hi Bob, come and have yourself a drink with your friends.' He was greeted with warmth and camaraderie and feeling generous, more drinks followed, mostly bought by him; and while his head became heavier his pockets became lighter.

At last it would be time to return home. Mrs Slessor would be waiting anxiously with the family by her side. She knew what to expect; it was a regular occurrence. As Bob lurched through the door she quietly enquired, 'Before you start your meal, ha'you any money from your wages for me? I need to buy more food for the family.'

'Money, money, money. That's all you think about. Do you begrudge me relaxing wi' me friends? Here, take this.' He threw down on the table all that remained from his week's wages—a few coins. Mrs Slessor knew she couldn't feed the family for a week on that small amount.

But without fail on the Sunday morning Mrs Slessor prepared herself and her six children for church, dressed in their poor best, the younger ones being given a peppermint to suck during the service. They left Bob to his misery and tiny garden which he tended on a Sunday, a sinful thing in that age and area. In the afternoon Mrs Slessor and the children gathered to sing hymns, read the Bible and talk about the missionaries in foreign lands. Mrs Slessor was a great supporter of the mission field.

There were eventually seven children in the family and Mrs Slessor had high hopes of Robert, the eldest becoming a missionary in one of the countries about which the family had read so much. Mary, spirited and lively with flaming red hair and a temper to match, also prayed that Robert would one day leave the cold Scottish climate and travel to the far ends of the earth to preach the gospel. He was the only one of the children allowed to go to school; there was no money for any of the others to be educated. It was hoped this schooling would equip him for a better future.

Mary was eight at this time and very mindful of the plans of her mother. Though even then she would have liked to be the one chosen to be a missionary, she realised it was not what women did.

'Mother, I would like to be a missionary too and go to the black children in Africa.'

'Girls can't be missionaries,' scorned her brother.

'It's far too dangerous for a woman,' her mother warned her. 'Your job is to stay here and help me look after your younger brothers and sisters.'

6

'At least no one can stop me dreaming,' Mary muttered to herself.

She contented herself by playing imaginary schools with her very few dolls; she always imagined them as black little children. Whenever she could she took her younger brother and sisters out into the countryside to gather the odd beautiful flower and rejoice under the Aberdonian sky. But these were rare occasions. As the oldest daughter, Mary was expected to assist her mother in cleaning the house, caring for the younger ones, lending a hand with the endless washing, ironing and shopping for the cheapest food.

On one occasion Mary asked her father to take them out for a walk; her mother was outraged. 'So he can lure you wi' his wicked ways while I slave to keep you all decent and respectable. No, go to your room and pray for forgiveness.'

Such discipline was necessary: it was vital to keep temptation away from her children. But while Mary was still in single figures and Robert sixteen, her brother was taken ill with a hacking cough. Day and night he coughed and seemed to grow worse.

'Please God, heal Robert so he can be a missionary for you,' Mary earnestly prayed.

But Robert grew weaker and suddenly died. Like the rest of his family after him, except for Bob and Mary, he died of tuberculosis for which there was no known cure at that time. Consumption, as it was also called, was a disease spawned by the poor living conditions of the city.

Broken-hearted, Mary cried, 'I'll tak' his place on the mission field.'

'Don't be silly child, it's a job for a man,' said Mrs Slessor as she began to nurture plans to train up her second son, John.

The tragedy of his son's death became too much for Bob. He drank more and more and due to his drunkenness was fired from his job. This made the task of feeding and clothing the family even more difficult, but surprisingly it was Bob who came up with a solution.

'Let's move and make a fresh start,' he suggested. 'I'll be away from my drinking friends and maybe I can find work in another town. I've heard there are openings in Dundee.'

'Yes, but what about *my* friends,' moaned Mrs Slessor. 'If we move I'll lose them and how can we afford it?'

Nevertheless after somehow managing to pay off all their debts the Slessor family found a place, known as a 'single end' in the city of Dundee. About 30,000 people lived in this inferior accommodation in areas where the streets were like open cesspits and the smells overpowering. As Mary held her nose against the stench she longed for Aberdeen, but there was no going back. The family had taken little with them as most of it had been sold to pay the outstanding debts. Fairly soon Bob found work again which had been the main purpose of the move.

Mary, now aged ten, had a playful disposition, probably linked to her flaming red hair as she tried to live up to her nickname 'Fire'. Apart from the smells and squalor, Mary eventually revelled in her new life. She soon found new friends, lively, but not too wild. She wasn't always good and serious; there was a mischievous side to her as well. One of the favourite games was to knock on people's doors and then run away before they could answer. The women of the city would be disturbed from their washing, ironing or another of their never-ending jobs to answer the door to non-existent callers. Mary and her friends were the bane of their lives. She once said, 'A little nonsense now and then is relished by the wisest men.' Maybe the door-openers wouldn't have agreed with her.

The city of Dundee was also blighted with the pollution of factories, but here they were mostly jute and flax ones.

Industrial smog hung over this town, causing illness, weakness and in many cases early death of the city's children.

One day Mary caught the eye of an old woman with 'a nose for sin' who lived on the edge of the town. She didn't believe in children enjoying themselves and playing games, especially Mary's wild ones. She called Mary and some of her friends into the cottage. Attracted by the warmth of the fire, the youngsters went it. Suddenly the old woman grabbed Mary's hand and held it near the blazing fire.

'D'ye see that! If ye were to put your hand into the flames they'd burn you sore. Repent, turn from your sins, or you will blaze in the fires of hell for ever and ever.'

Terrified, Mary tore her hand away and rushed home to throw herself down on her bed.

'What can I do? I'm a sinner?' she sobbed. She didn't want to burn in hell for ever. 'I repent, I repent,' she cried, 'I do believe.'

She sobbed herself to sleep and that night she temporarily lost a lot of her gaiety. For a while she refused to play with the other children and stayed close to her mother who was now recovering from the birth of her seventh child, baby Janie. Mary's added presence was a great help to Mrs Slessor at that time.

As Mary grew in her Christian life she learned from her mother to be thankful for what she had and to be thankful for what she didn't have. Her mother taught her, 'Thank God for what you receive. Thank God for what you do not receive. Thank God for the sins you are delivered from, and thank God for the ones you know nothing about and are never tempted to commit.'

Holding Mary's hand over the flames was a drastic way to convict a small child of her sin, but Mary came to learn that there is no conversion without repentance. The influence of her Christian mother and the intervention of the old woman affected her decision to follow Christ. She learned the truth of the Bible where it says in Proverbs, *'Train a child in the way he should go and when he is old he will not turn from it.'* She might not have been so happy with the text which says, *'Fathers, do not exasperate your children!'*

Bob Slessor was soon out of work again. This meant Mrs Slessor had to go out and find employment herself. She found a job working on a loom at Baxters, a local jute mill. This meant much of the care of the family fell on Mary. But before long these wages were not enough to keep the family and so in 1859 at the tender age of eleven Mary was also sent out to work. At Baxters Mill, one of the most successful textile firms that at one time had employed 5,000 workers, Mary became a half-timer which meant working for six hours at a noisy, clacking loom and then spending the rest of the day at the mill school. This was not unusual in this poor city; there was always plenty of work for the youngsters who were regarded as cheap labour.

'Mary, you'll find it noisy at first, but you'll soon get used to it,' Mrs Slessor explained. 'If you want to talk to your fellow workers, you must learn to lip-read.' She added: 'The good thing is that you can go to school when your shift is finished.'

'How exciting!' Mary exclaimed. 'I've always wanted to learn things like Robert was able to.'

The factory where Mary and her mother now worked manufactured products made from the jute. Jute is grown in the hot climate of the Ganges in India. Cultivated both on the highlands and lowlands, it is a reed-like plant which can grow 3-5 metres high. Preparation of the soil begins in the autumn and continues until the spring. The annual crop sowing takes place in February and June after the land has been suitably ploughed. The seed germinates at a fast rate and can grow up to seven centimetres a day. The harvesting takes place between July and October.

The plants are then cut down and laid on the ground to allow the stems to sweat and the leaves to fall off. These stems are then hit with a wooden mallet and swished to and fro in clear water to remove any remaining dirt.

The jute, classified according to colour, strength and fineness, is then tied into bundles with different graded bundles being placed in recognised overseas markets. Today many of these processes would be mechanised. In the 1800's the jute was sent to Britain for use in rope making, sacking, baling materials and increasingly in the ship-building industry.

Dundee, at the mouth of the River Tay, was the foremost port in the country for receiving this jute. In 1815 the harbour had been renovated and extended which made it easier to be used by the larger ships. The growth in the jute industry in Dundee in the second half of the 19th century was directly linked to the growing trade with India.

Dundee had an increasing tradition for building the large, fast ships which were needed to transport the jute from India and for the world-wide distribution of the finished goods. As the whaling industry had also increased there was plenty of whale oil which was needed in the preparation of the jute. All these factors increased the importance of Dundee.

Success came at a price. Of necessity conditions in the factories were not good. Poor wages were paid and the hours were long with the added danger of over-tired workers harming themselves on the fast moving machinery. (There were none of the Health and Safety Standards of today.) The general health of the city was bad. Cholera visited in 1832 and again in 1849. Smallpox was still found in Dundee when it had disappeared elsewhere and fever was always rampant. At the Baxters Mill, one of the better mills, a doctor visited every other day dispensing much needed medicine.

In 1817 boys aged 11-12 were gauged to be 4½ inches short than their contemporaries in the rural areas. Meat was a luxury, the main diet being potatoes and porridge. Bread and milk was served for dinner and tea.

In 1833 boys worked 18-19 factory hours a day; no wonder there were accidents. By 1863 it was reckoned that the average life span of a man was 33 years and a third of all children died before their first birthday. In 1882 conditions were even worse than in Glasgow—another industrial place. Dundee was a city where nearly 30,000 people existed in squalor.

In the mid-eighteen hundreds conditions in general, and for the Slessor family in particular, were poor. Such hardships were excellent preparation for Mary who would be spending most of her life in deprived conditions.

Chapter 2

MISSIONARIES FOR AFRICA

EVERY MORNING Mary would set off to work in her long wide skirt, with her shawl over her head and books tucked under her arm.

'Mother, I do so love being able to go to school,' Mary confided in her mother. 'There is so much I want to learn.'

She worked well at the mill and was soon controlling two 60-inch power looms. Because she was so fast at her work she was given permission to have her textbooks beside her loom. She would wedge them up against the vibrating machinery and snatch a moment of learning whenever she could. Come the end of the day, she eagerly went to the school to learn even more. She devoured every book in the Sunday School library, some of which were beyond her.

'I want to read all the books that have ever been written,' Mary made the impossible statement. 'I want to learn everything there is to learn.'

The family now consisted of Bob and Mary Slessor, Susan, John and Janie who was born when Mary was fourteen. Two other children had been born to the Slessors, though they died at a very young age. When alive they had added further to the financial burden of the already impoverished family. Mary's hours were then increased to ten followed by the hours of learning. She was still heart-broken by the death of Robert and as she studied the Bible further she became a gentler and more thoughtful person. But life for the family could never be the same again.

It was probably Bob who was most badly affected by the death of Robert. He drank more, was constantly out of work and suffered further bouts of ill health. It was only one year after they had left Aberdeen that his dissipated life caught up with him as he had one final illness and died. Although living with her father had been hard, Mary was grief-stricken. Her family seemed to be falling apart. Throughout this time Mrs Slessor remained firm in her faith and still sought single handed to bring up all her children as Christians.

As she mourned, Mrs Slessor realised that the Bob who had died was not the Bob she had married. She remembered with nostalgia the happy times they had experienced together before the children had been born and poverty had ground them down. But now the need for money to provide for the family was greater than ever. There were no benefits in those days. For a short while Mrs Slessor left the factory and ran a shop which meant she could spend more time with her family. Mary helped her whenever she could when her factory shifts were over, especially on Saturdays when the trade was at its busiest. Susan was now old enough to be working as a 'half-timer' and the family were able to move into a slighter better accommodation although it was still in a slum area.

Since Mary had become a Christian she loved to spend time with other Christians so that she could learn more about the God she loved. She became a Sunday School teacher and taught others what she was only just beginning to learn herself. She attended the Wishart Church which had been built near the old Port Gate in Cowgate. George Wishart had been burned at the stake for his beliefs in 1544 more than three hundred years before. The Cowgate was an area where poor girls and boys still roamed the streets, even a tough area for our little mill girl, who had a toughness of her own. 'Mary, I want you to speak at the meeting next Sunday,' requested James Logie, the minister of the church.

But Mary was painfully shy, mainly because of her hidden secret. Having had a drunk for a father, she felt she had no right to stand up and talk about the Lord. Although it had probably been an open secret, Mary was still deeply ashamed. She didn't want the neighbours to discover how Bob had come home drunk night after night; how he used to beat his wife and had spent his wages on drink which should have been used to feed his family.

A small mission had been started up in Queen Street, an even rougher area of slums, where the arched passages called Pends were full of poverty-stricken tenements. To this mission Mary went full of her pioneering spirit; for the whole of her life she never wanted to be with the posh, well-to-do people. There could have been no better grounding for a prospective missionary; the area and work gave her opportunity to tell the needy about her Lord.

Today, in this part of Dundee, there is a brass plaque to commemorate the life of this ginger-haired mill girl who went on to do great things for the Lord. Mary, her hair fashioned in short auburn ringlets, was a sight for sore eyes as she rushed hither and thither dispensing help and the gospel. It was not surprising that she earned the nickname of 'Carrots'. Her feisty character was directly related to her hair colouring giving her a temperament which in the years ahead would quell African chiefs and disturb British officials.

The whole of Mary's life was underpinned with love—love of the Lord and love for those needy youngsters. It was this love which won their acceptance and devotion. They were wild and noisy; not surprising, as they'd not had much discipline in their lives. Beatings, yes, but not true loving discipline. Mary always wanted to include these ruffians in her meetings but they didn't want to know about her and her God.

This was similar to the rejection she was to experience many years later in Africa. The Dundee lads thought she would spoil their fun, which was seldom innocent.

One evening a group of particularly wild lads laid in wait for her. As she appeared one of them advanced in a menacing manner. This was not the only time she was physically threatened but Mary was learning that to stand up to the bullies was to overcome them. As the bully swung his lead weight nearer and nearer to her ginger ringlets she prayed, 'Please, Lord, don't let me flinch, however scared I am. I do so want to win them for You.' That day the lad learned that flaming red hair equalled courage. After she had defied the lad and thereby succeeded in drawing them into the church, this particular group of lads followed her around and protected her from other unruly youths such as they had once been. Furthermore, they began to realise that Mary really cared about them.

Another convert she won through was a young lad who used to whip other young boys to make them go to the meetings. He pretended he was helping but actually the whipped youngsters were so frightened they never turned up again.

As Mary became exasperated with this behaviour she asked him, 'What would you say if we changed places and I used the whip on you?'

'Why, then you would have to beat me.'

'No,' she replied, 'I would then take the whipping in your place. Come on, whip me now.'

Disgusted, the boy threw down the whip and ran away. A few days later he came back, went to the meetings and eventually gave his life to Christ. Quite likely he never again used a whip in anger.

Years later in the steamy African jungle Mary was to use this ploy against a large drunken whip-welding native who was beating 'defenceless ones'. On that occasion Mary snatched the whip and attacked the 'whipper'.

After the death of Robert, Mrs Slessor's ambition of sending a son to the mission field was transferred to her second son, John. To this end he was given an apprenticeship as a blacksmith although the lack of his factory wage placed a severe burden on the family finances. However, as he was of a delicate disposition and the air in Dundee was not healthy, the family were advised to send him to New Zealand to improve his condition. He hadn't been there very long before the sad news came back to Scotland that soon after arriving he had died. The family were further saddened knowing that he had died alone in a foreign country.

Now that Mary mourned yet another brother she was all the more determined to become a missionary herself. Surely as her two dead brothers couldn't go, she must go herself. All her life had been hardship so she knew she could cope on the mission field.

Mary and her mother were avid readers of the *Missionary Record*, a magazine which told of missionary work all over the world. As each edition came out they would read it from cover to cover. Nothing happened on the mission field which had not been read about and discussed in the Slessor household.

'Were there any missionaries at the service tonight?' Mrs Slessor always asked when Mary returned home after the Sunday services.

'No,' sighed Mary, 'I do so love it when they come and tell us of their work. I especially liked hearing Mr Anderson from Calabar; he really made his stories come alive. I would so love to be there.'

Calabar was a principal slaving port in West Africa, whose trade had devastated the Efik tribes. John Buchan explained it so well in his *The Expendable Mary Slessor*—'The tribes all traded with one another. Some were farmers, some fishermen, some made canoes, some pottery and some wove raffia cloth, while a tribe of travelling blacksmiths practised their

17

metalwork skills. Tribes like the Efik even owned a few domestic slaves. It was a simple way of life that the slave trade destroyed.'

But was it where God wanted Mary to go? She'd read of India, Japan and Africa in her mother's missionary magazine but the place which really intrigued her was the Calabar in West Africa. She knew of the hardships, the slavery, the poverty and the killing of twins. She also knew it was a land of tropical jungles, wild animals, death, superstition, destruction and devastation.

'Please God,' she pleaded, 'will you send me to the Calabar to care for the black babies and tell the people of Your love?'

On the 4th May 1873 a telegram raced through Great Britain. David Livingstone, the great missionary and explorer, had died. In a small hut in the wild country of East Africa, Livingstone had breathed his last. Or had he? It wasn't unusual for David not to be heard of for months or even years as he'd explored the unknown African lakes and rivers and introduced the people to the thoughts of God.

The legendary life which he'd lived now threw doubt on the fact that the body was actually his. But there was proof enough. Many years earlier he'd been mauled by a lion and the severe fracture he'd received to his upper arm had never properly mended. He'd been fitted with a false joint between his elbow and shoulder though his arm still remained useless. This corpse had the same false joint. It was true: the great David Livingstone was dead.

Mary was devastated as he'd always been her hero. He'd been born thirty-five years before her, but there were many parallels in their lives. Both Scottish, David had been born on the 19th March 1813 in Lanarkshire and, like Mary, was the second child in a large family. He had worked for thirteen years, from the age of ten to twenty-three in a cotton mill, first as a 'piecer' (someone who tied the ends of the cotton together) and then a spinner, while Mary started work in a jute factory in Dundee at the even younger age of eleven, first as a 'piecer' and then as a 'loomer'.

Both were allowed to read and study while they worked, propping their books up beside their looms. David studied Greek and continued his Biblical studies while Mary increased her slight education by reading any book she could get hold of, even John Milton's *Paradise Lost* and works by Thomas Carlyle.

David had been sent out to Africa by the London Missionary Society as a qualified doctor and missionary but had also become investigator, imperial reformer, anti-slavery crusader and advocate of the commercial empire. At one stage he had to leave the missionary society as it was felt he was spending more time as an explorer than as a missionary; which no doubt was true.

David would never have known of the existence of this mill lassie; while Mary worshipped Livingstone from afar. His death was the inspiration to encourage her further in thinking that God wanted her to serve Him in Africa.

'I place no value on anything I have or may possess, except in relation to the Kingdom of Christ. If anything will advance the interest of the Kingdom, it shall be given away or kept, only as by giving or keeping it I shall promote the glory of Him to whom I owe all my hopes in time and eternity.'

These words of David inspired Mary.

In his obituary more of his words were quoted: 'I direct you to Africa. Do you carry on the work I have begun? I leave it with you.' Mary felt that this was a direct message from God; she could carry on the work, though in a very humble way.

David had also said, 'I am prepared to go anywhere, provided it be forward'—words which Mary was now echoing. She knew she couldn't be an explorer, nor did she feel the call to East Africa, but she knew there was missionary work to be done on that Dark Continent. Surely this was the time.

Her family were now settled, Mrs Slessor and Susan were both working, and the other children were growing up. David and Mary's lives could both be described as 'rags to riches'; rags of sin and the poverty of this world to the riches of the Kingdom of God.

These missionaries had been brought up to know and love God through their families and their churches, who had followed the adage, *'Tell your children and your grandchildren' (Exodus 10:2).*

In her approach to her future Mary took advice from her minister and Christian friends. She studied the Bible for more guidance; a practice she continued all her life. She prayed:

'Lord, make my future clear to me. You know I want to serve You as a missionary. Please make this happen.'

The next step was for Mary to apply to a missionary society. Would she be accepted? She knew she wasn't very well educated but the call to the mission field was strong. She also needed to know if it was the right time to leave her family. Susan was now working full time and Janie was old enough to work as a 'half-timer'. Mary's other question was whether Africa was the place God really wanted her to be. She had so many questions but not enough answers.

As she asked advice from her Christian acquaintances she received mixed answers.

'You're too timid to be able to cope with the rigours of that heathen country. In any case we don't want you to leave us.'

Others said, 'We know nothing will stop you going, if you really want to.'

She also turned to the scriptures for help:

> *'Go and make disciples of all nations, baptising them in the name of the Father and of the Son and*

of the Holy Spirit and teaching them to obey everything I have commanded you.' (Matthew 28:19-20.)

'It was He who gave some to be apostles, some to be prophets some to be evangelists and some to be pastors and teachers.' (Ephesians 4:11.)

God knew the end from the beginning. Mary knew she could never have left her family while her father was still alive. When Bob Slessor was drunk Mrs Slessor was in physical danger and often Mary had to intervene. Brothers Robert and John had been the first choices to be trained as missionaries but they had both died. With the death of David Livingstone, Mary felt more strongly than ever that it was now the time to go to the mission field. The four deaths had changed her situation and her thinking.

'Mother,' she announced eventually, 'I'm going to offer myself to train as a missionary. From my wages I will be able to send money home for you and the bairns.'

How delighted her mother was! She had dreamed of her two sons becoming missionaries, and now she was able to give Mary her blessing as she applied to the Foreign Mission Board of the Presbyterian Church. Would they accept her? They did. Three months of intensive training at Moray House in the Scottish capital of Edinburgh followed. After Dundee, Edinburgh seemed a very big place with its wide streets, posh shops in Princes Street and Gothic spires dotted round the city.

For the few months she was there she worshipped at Bristo Church while the whole city was still feeling the influence of the recent visit of D. L. Moody and the singer Ira Sankey. Mary was also excited to learn that Livingstone had previously visited this capital about twenty years before.

She became friendly with the McCrindle family, whose unmarried daughter and a friend inspired by Mary later became missionaries themselves in China. Many years later Mary was pleased to stay with the elder daughter and family on one of her furloughs.

Her acceptance was boosted by a glowing reference from her minister, James Logie back in Dundee. He had witnessed first-hand her fervour in winning souls and her aptitude for sheer hard work. Both would be required in the mission field. After training Mary made her application to the Foreign Mission Board but didn't state where she wished to go. She was learning that God's will was most important.

She qualified as a trainee teacher in early 1876 and was told, 'There is a pressing need for someone to go to the Calabar.' How she rejoiced and thanked God! This was the one place where she wanted to serve Him.

But Mary still had a lot to learn as she was only a partially educated mill worker. First she had to polish up her accent which was a mixture of broad Dundonian with lingering traces of her Aberdeen roots. She had to improve her English and Biblical knowledge. James Logie's wife taught her the social skills, which had been sadly lacking in her young life. Wryly, Mary didn't think there would be many drawing rooms in Calabar in which to practise these newly found skills.

'Does it matter which knife and fork I use? I just want to get enough to eat.'

When she received medical training, she privately questioned, 'Why do I need these skills? I'm going as a teacher, not a doctor.' She didn't realise then that every skill would be needed, that of doctor, nurse, builder, concrete mixer, teacher and advocate.

Some of her friends laughed at her; after all, when she saw a dog in the street she would cross over to avoid it. And now she

22

was proposing to go to the land of crocodiles, cannibals and baby killers!

Chapter 3

GOD'S CHOICE OF CONTINENT

MARY'S TRAINING TIME in Edinburgh was over all too soon. She was eager to go but frightened at the same time. One fear was that she would never see her family and friends again. She had been so appreciated at Wishart Church that she was presented with a gold watch and commenced her great adventure at the port of Liverpool accompanied by two men from the mission board. The journey was to be on the *SS Ethiopia* on the 5th August 1876. Aged nearly twenty-eight, Mary at last set sail for West Africa. Her last words on leaving her home town were, 'Pray for me.' Many prayers would be necessary both from herself and her friends. The continent to which she was going was known as 'the white man's grave'; even more a grave for women.

God had placed in Mary's heart the desire to go to Calabar but she had to learn to wait for His timing and to follow His will. It was only through obedience that Mary was going to be used by God.

'Created... to do good works, which God prepared in advance for us to do.' (Ephesians 2:10.)

Many years before Mary's time a slaver had sailed up the broad shallow estuary of the Calabar River to buy slaves at Duke Town, but the danger of the area from 'wreakers', those who wreck the visiting ships, made him afraid. Suddenly his vessel was caught in a tornado, so common in that area. At the same time he saw a canoe of cannibals bearing down on them.

The slaver, with his crew, abandoned ship and hid in the mangroves while the ship was looted and sunk.

Unable to go forward they hung on to the mangroves as long as they could, while mosquitoes and leeches attacked them. One by one the men slipped into the water and were lost to drowning or crocodiles.

'Keep yourselves cool by dipping yourselves in the water,' Dr Ferguson, the ship's surgeon advised, but they were trapped; the cannibals were still patrolling the area. Suddenly, Ferguson saw a lone canoe approaching.

'Keep quiet,' his men urged him. 'It's probably more cannibals.'

'But maybe it's from Duke Town and it's our only chance of survival,' he replied as he hailed it.

Fortunately Dr Ferguson was right. The ship took them to the local king where they were kindly treated, their burns dressed and medicines given to ease their fevers. Ferguson never forgot their kindness and thereon lost his taste for slaving and decided to use his skills on a packet ship between Liverpool and Jamaica.

While Ferguson was in the sugar plantations in Jamaica he noted that many of the slaves had come from the Cross and Calabar Rivers and he recalled the kindness he'd received while stranded in that area. As emancipation arrived the slaves also remembered their people back in their home towns and wanted to improve their conditions. Eventually funds were raised and the Scottish Missionary Society applied for permission to form a mission station at Calabar.

Ferguson, by now a rich Liverpool merchant, heard of their venture. He contacted the Calabar chiefs about the possibility of establishing this mission station and by 1843 ground was obtained to commence the work. Three years later missionary work started. In 1846 the Rev Hugh Waddell with a group of freed African slaves started work around the Calabar and Cross

River area. A mission was established on the hill above Duke Town and further missions started at Old Town, Creek Town, Eknetu and Okorofiong with ordained missionaries and a dozen or so lay teachers. It was going to be an uphill struggle as many long-established evils needed to be overcome, but it was a beginning.

As the shores of Britain disappeared and Mary dried her tears, she turned her thoughts to the future. Her twenty-eight years had all been spent in Scotland; she had learned little of the rest of the world. She was quite ignorant about and knew virtually nothing of the language of the country to which she was headed.

It was going to be a long journey—5,000 miles before they reached the coast of Africa. Mary was cheered up on the journey by meeting up with an architect, Mr Thompson and his wife, from Glasgow. He dreamed of building a mansion where weary missionaries could retire. He described the Calabar to Mary, the dense mud-coloured rivers with their seemingly never-ending lush green banks; the fierce sun, the wild animals, brilliant coloured flowers and bright plumed birds. But as they both knew, it was a region of great heathenism and idol worship. Mary wasn't deterred by his talk; she just realised all the more that these people needed God. Mr Thompson's idea to build this mansion was a good one but unfortunately he died before he was able to put his plans into practice. Mary kept this great idea in the back of her mind. Maybe she could eventually do something.

Mr Thompson had explained much more to her. The area of Calabar was divided up into Houses controlled by a freeman who exercised absolute control over slaves and wives. Houses owed allegiance to the king either of Duke Town or Creek Town. The native Efiks were the middlemen between the white British and tribes further inland, in regions such as

Okoyong and Ibo Ibibio, unknown to Mary at this stage but soon to become a vital part of her life.

Much of the area was controlled by the Egbo, a secret society based on ancestor worship who in their grotesque masks and bizarre costumes terrorized the region, stripping and scaring women or slaves in their path. Their craftily chosen fetish was the leopard, the most feared animal in the jungle. Only the rich slavers could afford 'to buy Egbo' which was supposed to give them protection. There were also rumours that there were further secret organizations known as Blood Men and Leopard Men. The result was that the Egbo controlled the trade routes so the bush men couldn't reach the whites and the whites couldn't reach the bush men. Their vigilante groups controlled the movement of trade between the interior of the jungle and the trading outposts.

The main commodity was palm oil. The 60ft palm trees had to be climbed to harvest the fruit. Clusters of the fruit were then lowered by ropes. Each mature tree could produce 600 pounds of bright red, tinged with black, fruits. The husks were then boiled to produce the palm oil which could be used for machine oil as well as the better grade oil used for cooking while the lower grade was used for making candles and soap. Often the natives drained sap from the trunk of the palm to make cheap gin for themselves. This lowered the yield of the fruit.

The first sight of the continent which Mary had was of Cape Verde, the westernmost point of Africa, and later she spied what she was told was Sierra Leone. Instead of continuing south the ship turned east and the horizon to the north was filled with land. The sea changed from a deep blue to a muddy brown, the effect of being joined by the Cross River which at that point was some ten miles wide with dense mangrove forests along each bank. The steamer then turned right into the Calabar River. This then was Africa and this was Duke Town,

Mary's first foreign home. The river became narrower so Mary could clearly see the pale fluted trunks of the mango trees, the prancing monkeys and brightly coloured parrots.

On 11th September 1876, after five arduous, seasick filled weeks, the *SS Ethiopia* steamed into the turbulent waters of this part of the African continent. Under the blazing midday sun and swaying palm trees, the cold northern shores of her homeland seemed very far away.

As Mary gazed at the hills in front of her she spied dozens of mud huts with what seemed like thatched roofs whose palm fronds quivered in the breeze. Long legged cranes and pelicans eyed the passengers warily while man-eating crocodiles slid off their mud-banks to cool in the murky waters. The sight took Mary's breath away as her nostrils were filled with the perfume of various spices and the odours of rotting fish.

'My first steps on African soil,' said Mary as she staggered on to the firm land. Then she silently screamed as she saw a six foot long snake-like beast sliding along the slipway.

'What's that?' she stammered.

'It's only a monitor lizard,' a sailor informed her. 'You'll need to get used to them in Africa. They make a lovely meal for the crocodiles.'

Mary shuddered; would she ever learn to accept the beasties of this continent? She also noted with sadness that numerous casks of liquor, rum and gin were being unloaded along with the passengers' luggage. She sighed. 'Scores of liquor casks, but only one missionary.' Mary was not to know then that this was the government's way of dealing with the stolen palm oil which was causing such loss of revenue.

Of course, Mary was not the only missionary, just one of the few, to disembark from the *SS Ethiopia*. The mission had only been in operation for some thirty years when Mary arrived and the work was being done mainly at Duke Town, Old Town and Creek Town some fifty miles up the Calabar River.

Occasionally some missionaries had ventured to open stations at Eknetu and Okorofiong but beyond that the area was unexplored. Mary's ambition knew no bounds but she tried to be patient and above all learn the many things she needed to know in this new work. But her first desire was to go deeper into the jungle and reach the tribes who hadn't been influenced by European ways.

When Mary arrived the team consisted of four ordained missionaries, their wives, eight teachers, eighteen African agents and one ordained African. Mrs Sutherland was one of the first missionaries to meet her. As Mary learned more about her, she found she was as fearless as Mary hoped to be. Other missionaries, Daddy and Mummy Anderson, also took over the task of looking after the new recruit. Mary well remembered Mr Anderson coming to Dundee to speak at the Wishart Church of his work here in Calabar. That had been one of the first stirrings for Mary to fall in love with the people here and she was delighted to be greeted by an old acquaintance.

She sighted the mission buildings up the hill and, nestling in the middle of the complex, was the school room. Mary was excited—this was where she would begin her work! Soon she would be teaching the African children whom she had dreamed of so long ago. Living high up on the hill above the noise and bustle of the town, these pioneer missionaries welcomed their young, exuberant and raw recruit. Mary was actually classed as a female agent; it would be some years before she was allowed to claim the name of missionary.

But at the time Mary's ginger hair still ruled her nature. Older and more circumspect missionaries looked on in dismay as very soon after her arrival she climbed trees and ran and played with the native children. She was soon able to confess to her friends back home, 'I've climbed every tree in the area that is worth climbing.' This was not what was expected of missionaries. She went about barefooted and whenever possible discarded many of her western petticoats. Indeed, she was considered to be too flighty to ever be able to make a success as a missionary. Time was to be the judge.

It was her job to ring the bell for morning prayers and sometimes she would mistake the brilliant African moon for the rising sun and ring while it was still night. The bell was supposed to be rung at five thirty in the morning; prayer was at six, a service at four in the afternoons and prayer again at six in the evening. Mary wasn't going to have much free time.

In spite of this her life was built on firm foundations and her faith was growing. *'She was like a tree planted by the water that sends out its roots by the stream.' (Jeremiah 17:8.)* She longed to start teaching these people about the love of God. The natives had been brought up in a culture which knew nothing about love. Gradually learning to be patient, she knew she would first have to learn the Efik language.

'This is a tonal language,' she was told. 'Whether you use a low, medium or high tone will change the meaning. At first you will make many mistakes. Depending on the tone, the word for chicken can also mean millstone or knife.'

Mary giggled; with her sense of humour she could envisage some funny errors and in her eagerness to learn tried to befriend some of the Efik women in the mission and walk with them to the market where she spent as much time as possible just listening. She found she was picking up the language very quickly and it was considered she was 'blessed with an Efik mouth.'

'Why are you always going down to the market?' she was asked.

'How else can I learn about the people and tell them about God? I don't want to spend my time in the mission compound. I want to get to know the people and understand their customs.' The markets were so different from any she had known in

Scotland. The produce on sale was mostly strange to her and she was anxious to taste various fruits.

Mary commenced teaching in the day school on Mission Hill, instantly loving the dark skinned boys and girls; she'd spent so much of her short life longing to be with them. The older children wore red and white shirts, the young ones nothing at all and they all carried their slates safely in their thick woolly hair. Most of her first charges were boys and initially they were afraid of her, but her love and concern soon won them over. It was a talent she displayed to all for the rest of her life. The children conferred on her the name of 'Ma', a title she was proud to accept.

Mary also earned the opportunity to visit the children in their own mud huts, places she preferred to be, as she found some of the missionary wives were quite smug in their attitude towards the people.

She was mesmerized by the African sunrises. The humidity of the night sky seeped away as the sun rose higher into the deep blue sky. Beauty was all around. She marvelled at the intense colours of the flowers and shrubs. Her Scottish eyes had never seen such brilliance. The birds with their vibrant colours fascinated her as they darted to and fro. No sparrow or blackbird from Dundee had ever looked like these.

The current history of the Calabar was that some progress had slowly been made from the evil practices. By 1852 slave sacrifice was classed as murder and guilt could no longer be established by a poison trial but these laws were not always adhered to, especially deeper in the jungle. The death of a chief occasioned widespread bloodshed.

In 1855 when Chief Willy Tom Robins of Old Town died, two of his sons and one of his wives died by poison, four wives were strangled and fifty slaves butchered. As this was against the law the missionaries demanded the murders were punished but the Old Town refused. Drastic measures were then taken.

After removing all the inhabitants, the *SS Antelope* attacked Old Town and burnt it to the ground. Duke Town then became responsible for the refugees which put an added burden on an already busy town.

A few years later permission was given to rebuild the Old Town so long as the evil ways were no longer practised. But an old alcoholic Duke Ephraim 'blew Egbo' on the mission and tried to starve the missionaries out. Intervention was necessary from the British Foreign Office with the arrival of *SS Scourge* and after a palaver (an African style meeting) with the reigning African king, peace was restored.

The worst of the atrocities were now only taking place deep in the jungle where Mary longed to go. She badgered the authorities for this move but was told it was no place for a white woman. The patience which she had learned at her looms now helped her to wait.

Three years in the harsh African climate began to take its toll. The 'harmatten', often known as the 'smokes', which usually arrived in late June, was a dust-bearing wind from the deserts of the north. These winds in June 1878 affected Mary badly and she felt even worse the next June. The doctor announced: 'You're not suffering from the effect of the harmatten, you have jungle fever.' She was placed on a steamer the very next week and returned to Scotland for a period of recuperation. A missionary was supposed to spend five years on the mission field before they had their first furlough, but Mary was so ill this rule had to be broken. In 1879 this was to be the first of her five visits back to her homeland.

On reaching England the mission board had insisted she travel by train from Liverpool to Dundee. This surprised her as she had expected to sail straight to Scotland and not use an English port. As she approached her hometown she knew why. The Tay Bridge just over two miles long had been completed the previous June and she was able to approach Dundee with a view she had never seen before.

But the history of the Tay Bridge was to be short-lived. Completed June 1878, it was a wonderful feat of engineering, but during a terrible storm on 28th December 1879, while Mary was still in Dundee, the bridge collapsed taking with it about 75 lives. If Mary had been on that ill-fated train the history of Calabar would have been very different.

It was a sick Mary who arrived back in the hometown. Jungle fever, malaria and dysentery had laid her low. But before long the love, care and good cooking of her mother built up her strength.

'My, how Susan and Janie have grown!' Mary exclaimed. 'You are quite young women now.' So much had happened to her family and friends in the absent three years. Some had married, some had moved away while others had additions to their families and older ones had died. It was hoped Mary could have a time of relaxation but that would not have been Mary's way. In any case the missionary society wouldn't allow that; many of her days had to be spent in deputation work.

Her fear of speaking to audiences who were more educated than her was still with her. She was especially scared of speaking to a male audience. Although her father had been dead for many years, his influence probably accounted for this. She needed to dig deep into the resources of God to give her strength. But once her shyness was overcome she was a captivating speaker as the stories she had to tell were riveting to her audience.

Chapter 4

FAMILY AND FURLOUGHS

BACK IN SCOTLAND on her furlough, there was great interest in the work which she had been doing in Calabar, especially as she had been in the country which was then known as 'the Dark Continent'. What were the people like? What about the insects and the wild animals? Were the people really cannibals? The Scottish people found it difficult to imagine what it was actually like in Africa. Conversely, Mary had become so acclimatised to life in Calabar that she now found everything very difficult in Dundee. She especially noticed that Scottish worship was more restrained. In Africa the services were joyful affairs.

Whenever Mary went to a meeting she was expected to speak, something which had never been easy for her. Time and again her shyness surfaced. It was strange that this wee lassie could face the brutality and threats of the African jungle and of the Africans themselves, but among her own people she was reticent. She was usually persuaded to say a 'few words', mainly by turning away from the audience and with her head bent low. But even these few words caught the attention of her listeners. As she spoke she forgot her temerity, her voice became strong, her face glowed with excitement and the life in Africa became real in the minds of these who heard her speak.

But Mary was becoming homesick—homesick for Africa, that is. Although the congregations in Scotland sang their praises to the Lord it was done in a solemn manner, often through psalms. Mary longed for the exuberance of the Africans, where the people sang and swayed to the rhythm of the music with hands held high in exaltation.

Mary's time on furlough wasn't just taken up with meetings. She realised that although her mother had lovingly nursed her back to health, Mrs Slessor was in poor health herself. One of Mary's urgent tasks was to move the family to a healthier part of the city. Finding a place in Downfield on the north-west side of Dundee, she was happy to transfer her mother and sisters, Janie and Susan. Janie was especially poorly, but at least they were away from the worst of the city pollution. It did mean that Mary would now have to spend more of her yearly salary of £60 to buy the house, but as she intended to live even more frugally it was a small price to pay for the improved health of the family.

Mary recognised it as a Biblical commandment to care for fathers and mothers. She knew that the sixth commandment in Exodus said *'Honour your father and your mother, so that you may live long in the land the Lord your God is giving you.'* No longer could she care for her father, but what she was able to do for Mrs Slessor, Janie and Susan, was part of her loving duty towards God.

When Mary's furlough was up, she requested to the Church Mission Committee that she be sent onto an outstation where the influence of missionaries had yet to be felt. She wanted to move to Okoyong which was upstream of Calabar and where slave sacrifice still continued. The Andersons were against this move. They considered Mary to be a first-timer who was pushing herself forward. Pioneers are not always easy to work with but they do become pioneers who can be used by God. It seems Mary was set to become one of these.

In the autumn of 1880, Mary was told, 'You will be sailing back to Calabar with Rev and Mrs Goldie.'

Then she was further told, 'You will be returning to Old Town.'

Mary was delighted. Old Town was two miles up the Calabar River. It wasn't the deep jungle she was hoping for, but it was a step in the right direction, especially as she would be in charge and on her own. She could now make some of her own decisions and there would be the added advantage that her fellow missionaries couldn't continue to be scandalised by her behaviour.

Travelling back to Africa with the Rev Goldie, Mary learned he was well versed in African affairs and particularly in the Efik language. He was to become noted for his Efik dictionary as well as standard Efik works.

Returning to Africa meant returning to African weather. One troublesome feature was the tornado. Mary found that those which arrived in Old Town were just as violent as those experienced in Duke Town. The climate back home in Scotland now seemed so tame compared to the wild weather of Africa.

'Don't stand outside in the rains,' Mammy Anderson ordered as Mary had experienced her first tornado, 'You'll be blown over.'

Having known fierce winds in Scotland, Mary didn't think this was possible but soon had to change her mind. The sky darkened and the thunder rolled. Gusts of rain pummelled down on the building where all the shutters had been drawn; it was so noisy on the tin roof it was impossible to hold a conversation. Leaves and twigs were hurled to the ground and even whole trees were uprooted as the wind tore at everything in its path. Fortunately, tornados didn't occur all the year round. The dangerous months were May to October.

Since Old Town had been blasted out of existence by *SS Antelope*, it had been rebuilt but had never fully recovered. Here Mary established some outposts from the town and filled her days with teaching, preaching, administering first aid and dispensing medicines. Her medicines were only quinine or painkillers. Advice she had once been given was 'use no native medicines, employ no native doctors, drink no rum, pray to Jesus for a blessing and praise Him for recovery.' The last three pieces of advice were easy to follow, but she did grow to appreciate the healing properties of some indigenous plants.

In the Old Town a small disused hut was found for her to live in which consisted of a framework of poles interwoven with small branches and the walls plastered with mud. Living here Mary could save even more money to send home to her family. With her loving and caring nature, the inhabitants of Old Town grew to love her as she lived with them, adopted their lifestyle and became one of them. She ate groundnut paste, dried fish, yams and manioc. She wore a tent-like garment which kept her cool under the fierce African sun. No conventional 'stays' for her. She went barefooted unless she went into Duke Town and, regardless of fashion, had her hair cut short. She had none of the standoffishness of some missionaries—no wonder she was loved by the natives!

Mary ventured to other villages: Kwa, Akim and Ikot Ansa. She taught the women and children, administered medicine and on Sundays conducted services. The sounds of her rich Scottish voice and playing of her organ penetrated the jungle confines.

The lack of free trade was one of the problems worrying Mary at this time. The greedy, selfish men in the towns wouldn't let the natives trade their palm oil with the factories, thus denying them a living. As a result fighting often broke out between Kwa and Efik tribes. The Ibo, a tribe who terrorized the region, continued to extend their influence further, making trading even more difficult. Mary sorted out the problem by allowing the natives to creep through the mission compound after dark to deliver oil to the factories. Before long the traders realised they couldn't outwit this fiery highland lassie and so a certain amount of free trade was established. Once again Mary had won.

Still Mary's desire was to go further into the jungle where unknown evils were continuing to be practised. She sometimes managed to venture further up the river by taking some of the Africans with her. On these occasions she 'went native', completely abandoning her European ways. She was able to visit chiefs who had come to know about her work and respected her for what she did. It was slow work but she was gradually gaining the Africans' confidence.

Eyo Honesty VII was the king of Creek Town who had become a Christian through missionary influence. He was very kind to Mary and often loaned her the use of his state canoe which was highly decorated and rowed by thirty-three oarsmen dressed only in loin-cloths. This Scottish missionary was certainly travelling in style.

Mary found the barbaric customs of the natives difficult to accept and tried to eradicate them wherever possible. Guilt of any crime was decided by taking poisonous beans. If the accused died he was obviously deemed guilty. A very small minority of miscreants managed to sick up the drink before it took effect. In this case they were considered innocent.

Another strange custom was that slave girls were made to grow very fat, as in this region plumpness was regarded as beautiful. The result was the poor girls could hardly walk and died of various diseases at a young age. Another custom which was barbaric was that when a chief died his wives would be strangled, their heads cut off and their bodies buried with his corpse.

On one occasion Mary was a guest of yet another chief, who was not as civilized as Eyo Honesty VII. Chief Okon, of the village of Ibaka, had discovered that four of his wives had gone into another yard to visit a young man. Okon decided that the punishment should be a hundred stripes, then have salt rubbed into the wounds and maybe have the ears of the offenders cut off—all this for just straying into a yard which was not their own. On this occasion Mary was able to use cunning and wisdom to defuse the situation.

'Bring the girls to me,' she said to the chief. Addressing the girls, she said, 'Yes, girls, you have done wrong and you must be punished, but it is only a small thing you have done wrong. You will have ten lashings only and no salt rubbed into the wounds.'

She then turned to the chief with anger in her eyes. 'You have done the greater wrong. You have married these young girls when they should still be having fun. You too must be punished.'

This was not to the chief's liking, but Mary was a guest and had to be treated with respect. Mary never recorded if the chief received any punishment.

In 1881/2 Mary's work was inspected. It seemed she couldn't always have her own way. The Foreign Mission Board in Edinburgh sent out two inspectors to check on the quality of her work, but happily they were able to report that she was a 'devoted and energetic agent and sustains her manifold duties cheerfully.' The recommendation was that she should be allowed to continue working alone in the Old Town 'because she prefers this manner of life to being associated with another person on a station'.

Later Mary found out that this inspection had been initiated because Alexander Ross, a fellow missionary who had been one of the first to welcome her to Africa, had complained about the Andersons and Mary's tolerant attitude to the natives. When the report came out Ross was angry and set up his own church nearby, causing the Efik to think there were two white gods in Duke Town. Fortunately the life of the rival church was short-lived.

Mary again received an invitation from King Okon to visit him and again had the use of King Eyo Honesty VII's canoe, complete with the thirty-three oarsmen. The journey was a dangerous one and took days. As well as the oarsmen, Mary was not alone. Parts of her journey were accompanied by massive lizards, many insects, stampeding elephants along the shoreline and huge constrictor boas waiting to attack the small vessel. But the opulent canoe meant she was able to arrive safely and with dignity.

On the return journey the party was overtaken by a severe hurricane. The skies darkened and the thunder crashed directly overhead. Torrential rain fell and the canoe was tossed about like a matchbox. The party was forced to paddle into the mangrove swamps, hang on to the overhanging branches to steady the canoe and wait for the storm to pass. When towards dawn the storm had subsided, they continued on their way, but Mary was drenched to the skin and fever and ague set in. The rowers were desperate to get her back to the safety of her own hut. But even then there was not much help as the storm had taken the roof off the mission building and she had to live in a trader's hut next door. Before long she was so ill she had to be taken to Duke Town. But it was too late. Her severe condition meant that it was again recommended she return to Scotland to recover.

In planning her return there was a problem. One of Mary's main tasks in Africa was rescuing twins who would otherwise have been killed by the superstitious natives. She had taken into her care two twins and she decided to take Janie, the little girl with her, back to Scotland. Therefore in April 1883 Mary and Janie sailed for her homeland.

The visit was an especially important time for little Janie. On a bright Scottish morning in Wishart Memorial Sunday School she was baptised as Jean Annan Slessor, known as Janie. What a sight she was with her black skin and solemn eyes taking in everything around her. She became everyone's favourite as boys and girls alike begged to hold her. She continued to appear at all the meetings where Mary was speaking and sat quite happily on the platforms munching biscuits.

While Mary was in Edinburgh she had to continue her much-dreaded deputation work, but it was to have good results. A young lady, Jessie Hogg, expressed to Mary that she would very much like to work with her in Africa.

'Then apply to the Board,' Mary urged. This is just what she did and very quickly she started medical training. In fact she was actually working in Africa before Mary's delayed return to that country.

One time when Mary was speaking in Falkirk her message made such an impression on her listeners that, guided by a Miss Bessie Wilson, people started to contribute money each month to support Janie. Thus fund-raising began. At the same time six members of the church pledged themselves to work in Calabar. In due course these young ladies were able to support and befriend Mary and the other missionaries in West Africa.

Unfortunately this was not a happy time for Mary as her return to Calabar had to be delayed. Two of her younger siblings had already died, and now sister, Janie, was ailing with consumption. This was an illness so prevalent at this time, caused by the poor living conditions of the slums. Regretfully, Mary had to give up all thought of returning to Africa in the near future. She did think of taking sister Janie back to Africa with her, but the mission board would not hear of it. A Presbyterian woman in Exeter suggested that Mary moved the family down there as the south of England would be so much warmer for the invalid. A cottage was found for them in the village of Topsham by a deacon of the Congregational Church where they were able to worship and they all moved down there. This house had a small garden which would have reminded Mary of her father who chose to work in his garden instead of attending worship. Mary resigned her post as a missionary in order to nurse her family, but she was held in such high regard that she was assured a place would be held open for her should her circumstances change.

For a short time Mary worked at the Exeter hospital to provide much needed funds for the family. She also considered the medical experiences would be useful if she was ever able to return to Africa.

Sister Susan, who had decided to remain in Scotland, died suddenly at the end of 1883 in Edinburgh while visiting the family friend, Mrs McCrindle. Mary hadn't realised how ill she had been and felt pangs of guilt and grief at her death. But it had been the young lady's wish to remain in the north, so there was nothing Mary could have done. With her death Susie's financial contribution to the family also ceased.

Meanwhile, Mary was gradually able to nurse Janie back to health. So the time came when she felt free to return to Africa. It was arranged that a friend from Dundee would travel down to care for the family. Nevertheless it was with a sad heart that she planned to sail. In returning she was afraid that this would be the last time she would see her family, but she needed to return to the Africa she loved and where the Lord was using her. On 11th November 1885 Mary and African Janie sailed back.

When Mary returned she was delighted to have the help of Miss Edgerly and Mrs Johnstone. Now she was stationed in Creek Town, a little further up the river from Old Town. She managed to live even more frugally so as to be able to send more money back to her family in Devon. But on New Year's Day 1886, only seven weeks after her return, the news came which she had been dreading. Her mother had died of tuberculosis. The godly woman who had taught her so much about the Lord had gone. This blow was followed a few months later with the news that Janie had also died. Now all her family were dead; this meant she had no relatives to call her own. It was a sorrow from which she never fully recovered. Now she was alone in the world, except for the Lord and her growing African family.

Always having a positive attitude to life, she realised she was now free from any family responsibilities. She had the freedom to go as deep into the jungle as she would be allowed to go.

Mary always wanted her work to bear fruit; she wasn't just a social worker trying to improve conditions in Africa. She wanted them to know about the love of God and was always striving towards that end. She took up to twelve services on a Sunday, explaining the love of God to the natives and the need to accept Him into their lives. Although she was pleased when twins became more acceptable or the chief's wives had better conditions, her real joy was when 'one sinner repented.' Spiritual fruit was essential to her life and work.

Mary's African family was growing. More surviving twins were being found. Her bed was always being shared by a number of tiny babies. The older children learned to help the younger ones. Food, time and love were all shared while the natives were still afraid of twins and kept out of her way. Other children had been saved from slavery and sickness and they also joined the family. All were trained to do housework, bake and go to market. They learned to read and write the Efik language.

Chapter 5

TWIN TRAGEDIES

WHILE MARY was still in Scotland working at her looms she had learned of the plight of twins in Calabar. The horror never left her. She thought it strange that when she was first in the country of Africa she didn't meet many twins but she soon realised it was because so many of them had been killed. The natives in Calabar hung on to their superstitions and devil worship and the killing of twin babies was the one custom which Mary fought against the hardest and for which she is best remembered.

It seemed that in this part of Africa the incidence of multiple births was higher than average and it was thought that twin births were the work of evil spirits. The belief was that one of the babies must have been conceived by the devil and the natives didn't know which one it might be. The Efik therefore decided that both babies must be killed. There were various inhumane ways of doing this, but the most common was to break the babies' backs at birth, crush their bodies into a calabash shell and then leave the pots out in the jungle to be attacked by wild animals. The mothers of these unfortunate offspring were often driven out of their homes into the bush as well, usually to follow the fate of their babies—death.

'Jesus said suffer the little children to come unto Me,' Mary said. 'I shall fight this horror; it must be stopped. I will never give up.'

This was to become a life work for Mary. Eventually the practice was outlawed though often the law was flouted and on many occasions Mary put her own life on the line to save as many twins as she could.

'How common are multiple births?' she enquired.

'About one in a hundred.'

This savage killing was an anathema to Mary and she very quickly started to address the problem. Often the mothers would murder one of the babies themselves and then pretend the surviving child was the result of a single birth. But on other occasions they were discovered and both babies killed. There are numerous stories of how Mary tried to combat this atrocity and she became well known for her compassion towards these mothers. Each rescue would have remained vivid in her mind as she extended her compassion.

Quite early on in her life in Calabar a trader arrived in the middle of the night carrying a bundle of filthy rags.

'What have you there?'

'A baby abandoned in the forest. If I had left her there she would have been eaten by wild animals. Alerted by the cries, I just found it lying under a bush. Her back hasn't been broken but she must be a twin. I knew you would like to keep the baby.' He handed Mary the small bundle of rags with a traumatised baby girl hidden inside.

Then the trader said in a stage whisper, 'I found her brother too, he is still alive.'

So Mary began her extended family. The little girl she named 'Janie' after her youngest sister and the boy when he was brought to her 'Robby' after her dead brother. By using these names she felt nearer to her Scottish family. When she returned to Scotland for her second furlough in 1883 she took this Janie with her while Robby was left in the care of a trusted family. Nevertheless when she returned to Calabar she discovered her helpers had been tricked into handing Robby back to his family and by now he was undoubtedly dead. A few years later the story had a happy ending. Janie's father came to see his daughter and through Mary learned to love her and continued to bring her little gifts.

The love which Mary was displaying she had learned from her Master and through the Bible. There are numerous examples of love and kindness in the Bible. Ruth the Moabite, through the love towards her mother-in-law, left her country and by marriage to Boaz came into the line of King David.

David showed the same kindness to Jonathan's surviving relative because of the covenant he had made with Jonathan himself. Mephibosheth was allowed to eat at his table and had all his land restored to him. This was a forerunner of God's invitation for us to eat at His communion table.

During her life Mary had received love and kindness from her mother, from Rev James Logie and from the missionaries when she first arrived in Africa. This was now the love of God which she was displaying to others. She loved the babies, she loved the mothers, and even loved those who opposed her or put her life in danger.

Mary's connection with Janie continued all her life. Janie grew up to be a lovely young lady and on the 21st December 1899 married Akibo Eyo who, it was thought, did not seem to worry that she was a twin. They lived with Eme Ete but sadly their baby died and Akibo felt that it was due to the fact that his wife was a twin and consequently left her. Janie's story didn't end there. She returned to Mary, was reliable and helpful with her work and continued even after Mary's death.

But Mary's concern for abandoned babies continued. Before long another child was found discarded in the forest with the body of the mother lying nearby probably having been killed by wild animals. When Mary got to the baby it was a wonder it hadn't been killed itself by a passing leopard. Even so, the poor mite had been attacked by insects and part of her nose eaten away. Eventually Mary was to nurse this baby back to health and she was regarded as a miracle baby who became known as 'Little Mary'.

In another story a mother of twins, knowing that her babies would be killed if she stayed with the family, fled to the jungle and then brought them to Mary. Having been exposed to the harsh elements, the little boy died very soon afterwards but the girl thrived under Mary's loving care and Iye, the mother, remained to live with Mary. They named the baby 'Susie' after Mary Slessor's sister.

On one particular day, another little girl was getting Susie ready for bed when the small child managed to spill a jug of boiling water over her bare body. The burns were horrendous. Mary nursed her faithfully for two weeks, hardly letting the baby out of her arms; but eventually they had to take her to a doctor at Creek Town. There was nothing that could be done; the shock of the scalding had been too severe. Poor Susie died. Mary's heartbreak at her death was overwhelming and she took a long time to recover from it. Even after both her babies had died, Iye remained as a faithful helper to Mary; there was no possibility of her returning to her family.

Okin was a little boy who had been handed to Mary's care by the mother's mistress, as the mother, a slave, had no say in her son's upbringing. Mary insisted that the boy should be brought up as a Christian but he was a difficult child to rear.

Another young boy named Ekim also joined Mary's growing family; he was a freeperson and possibly the heir to Old Town. Another child placed into Mary's care was Inyang, a large, very helpful thirteen year old who had no family although it was believed that her mother, Annie, had been cursed and had been a slave to one of the King Eyo Honesty's daughters. But Inyang was wanted by no-one. With all the others she became part of Mary's family.

Mary was kept so busy that she had little time to grieve for her own mother and sisters but she kept very safely her mother's wedding ring, which Janie had been able to send to her before her own death. Mary kept this as a keepsake.

Another mother of twins had run away into the jungle to flee from the wrath of the other wives. In their fear and superstition the natives had threatened to kill her and her babies. Mary ran the four jungle miles to find the distraught woman as she lay cowering in the jungle sheltering from the angry mob who were still trying to grab the twins. Mary forced her way through the howling crowd, scooped up the frightened family and took them all to the shelter of her hut knowing that the villagers were too superstitious to follow along the track she had taken. The local chief, who was usually kindly disposed towards Mary, was dismayed to know that twins had been taken to the hut so close to his own.

'Now I'll never be able to go to Mary's hut again,' he moaned.

Mary ordered him to come to her but such was his fear that he refused. For a time Mary was ostracized by the chief and the villagers, her Sunday services only receiving poor attendances. Very soon one of the twins died. The mother and the remaining twin continued to stay with Mary. Before long the chief felt guilty at his behaviour and sent Mary a head-load of yams by way of apology. Mary refused to accept them and sent them back. The chief was offended and went to see her in spite of his twin phobia.

'How can you reject my gift? Are we not your children?'

'Then behave like my children. Is not this mother and baby also my children? You must believe the Word.'

'We do want to believe the Word. Eventually we will believe it, but you must be patient with us.'

Mary sighed.

Eventually the chief said, 'If you say the twin is good, then it is good.'

There was a happy outcome to this story. In due course the father came to collect his wife and the twin, also bringing gifts for Mary. It was proving a long hard battle to win these people over, but on this occasion Mary felt she had made a little headway. The battle to rescue twins was one of the most difficult fights she ever had to undertake. Patience was what was needed and the power of prayer.

Patience was something she had needed all her life. When she was working in the jute mill back in Dundee it was easy to feel impatient when all she wanted was to be working as a missionary in Africa. When she did arrive in this continent she wanted to move further and further into the jungle as she knew the people there needed the gospel. But the authorities were always urging caution and taking time to make decisions on her behalf.

Mary was able to recall stories where people in the Bible had been called on to exercise patience—Abraham, Hannah, Joseph, Jesus and the apostle Paul. It was Paul who once said, *'Clothe yourselves with compassion, kindness, gentleness and patience.'* God's timing is not our timing but it is much more effective.

Mary heard of a woman in Ekenge who had given birth to twins and learned of the arguments within the family about the killing of these babies. Mary argued with the father to send the poor wee mites to Duke Town but it was to no avail. The killing was all planned.

'I have no time to lose,' Mary said to herself and knew there was only one thing to be done. She waited until the dead of night and then crept round to the back of the hut. As she heard a whimper she knew the babies were still alive. Quietly she started to make a hole in the wall of the hut and, reversing backwards, extracted the babies one by one. At this stage they started to scream alerting the whole family. With her bundles tucked safely under her arms she began to run and outran the family until she reached the safety of her own hut. Safely inside, she posted Janie outside to explain that the family couldn't come in and Mary wouldn't release the babies. The next day Mary noticed that the mother was still hanging around outside the hut while the rest of the family had gone home. Mary handed a bottle to this woman who gladly gave it to one of the babies.

In spite of all the loving care from Mary and Janie, within a few days one of the babies died. The natives thought it must have been the evil-possessed twin who had died and returned to visit Mary and accepted the surviving twin. Mary was so saddened; the superstitions were very hard to break.

Whenever a baby died, Mary treated it with reverence. The custom had been just to throw the body away. By contrast, Mary placed them in a little box with flowers before burying them. She valued even those who had not survived.

For the rest of her life Mary continued to collect unwanted babies whether they were twins or not and she was seldom without a baby in her arms and toddlers tugging at her skirts. At one time her family were counted and she was found to have seventeen babies and young children, most of them rescued twins.

As the years went by attitudes were to soften and some twins were accepted back into their families. Mary's heart rejoiced; this was what she had been working for all along. She realised that the problem of the killing was so entrenched in the history and culture of the people that even with legislation she couldn't solve it by herself. She recommended that a special person be appointed to deal with the issue. But more patience was needed as the Mission Board didn't listen to her and such a person was never appointed. It seemed as if she would have to continue dealing with the problem herself as best she could.

Chapter 6

INTO THE JUNGLE

MARY WASN'T SATISFIED with her progress to influence the people from their evil ways and bring the gospel to them. Her continual cry was that she wanted to work deeper into the jungle. 'I need to get to the root of these evils,' she said, 'to be able to stamp them out.'

The Okoyong region held a special attraction for her. Lying between the Calabar and Cross Rivers, beyond Creek Town the area was ruled by a warlike tribe, the Ebo (Ibo), who were feared by all around. It seemed as if they were perpetually drunk on gin, meaning lawlessness was rife. Mary pleaded with the missionaries at Duke Town that she should be sent there.

'No, no, it's far too dangerous, especially for a white woman who is on her own,' said the authorities.

'It's a gun boat they need, not a missionary,' the traders said.

Mary knew this was wrong but it was difficult for her to display the fruit of the Spirit and be patient. For about sixteen years she'd worked in the factory in Dundee and now she had worked for over ten years in the Calabar. How could she remain patient? Then suddenly she was told, 'We have news for you from the mission board. You have permission to go to Okoyong.' But it was made clear that it was *her* decision and that the mission station was clear of all responsibility if anything happened to her. The dangers were so great they were afraid they would never see her again.

Then came a blow. Everything was arranged for her go but the natives didn't want her. This so reminded her of the young lads back in Dundee who didn't want her interfering in their lives. The message of the Gospel is often unwelcome.

'We don't want any missionary, man or woman. They will make us change our ways. We want to remain as we are.'

The Okoyong people were different physically from the Efik; they were taller and had finer features. Although Mary had thought they were all alike, she now realised how different they were. For a whole year negotiations were carried out but no progress made. Palavars were held but to no avail. Early in 1888 a palaver had established one of the chiefs concerned: Chief Edem was prepared for her to come. Mary prepared to travel to Ekenge in the very heart of the Okoyong, but nothing further happened. Eventually Mary grew so impatient that she could wait no longer.

'I will go. I won't wait to be invited.'

In June 1888 arrangements were made for the journey. Again she had the use of the royal canoe and thirty-three oarsmen as they travelled towards the settlement of Ekenge. The river journey itself was an experience; water creatures were always nearby threatening to overturn the canoe. After the harrowing water journey she left the canoe and walked the four miles through a nearly impenetrable tangle of jungle growth, along uneven paths with the ever present danger of snakes and other wild animals.

After the four miles, the small party were surprised by groups of sentries, who were themselves amazed to see the strangers. They seemed awestruck and full of admiration for this little white lady who'd ventured so far into the jungle. A further surprise awaited her. Against her expectations as she entered the compound she was welcomed.

'Where are you going?' the natives asked the party.

'We've been invited to Ekenge. Are we at the village now?'

'No, only the chief lives here. He is safe here away from his tribe, but even so must sleep with machetes and guns by his side.'

Mary realised yet again what dangerous tribes she would be encountering. She was then introduced to the chief and dozens of his court officials. Unbelievably, the chief Edem was sober but he wouldn't allow her party to travel further as the men in the next village were drunk and therefore dangerous. She had to stay the night outside Ekenge.

When she first met Chief Edem he had by his side his sister, Eme Ete who seemed extra kindly disposed towards Mary and her companions. Mary and Eme were to be friends for many years, but although Eme was always polite, she never wished to embrace the faith which Mary preached. That evening Mary was allowed to hold a service and when she eventually reached her insect-infected bed she gave thanks to God for the welcome they had all received.

The next morning Mary explained to Edem her plan to open a mission at Ekenge, build a church, a mission house and a school house. Next day Mary travelled to Ifako, only half an hour's walk away where she was again able to explain her building plans and her thoughts of also building a sanctuary, which she wanted to be a refuge where people could be safe. She was amazed she had been able to give her proposals so quickly.

The friendship between Mary and Eme grew and they became like sisters. Eme would tactfully guide her brother on decisions he should be making and she also helped Mary to sniff out evil practices and inform her of the dangers.

Chief Okon who lived in the village near to Ibaka, down the great estuary on the far west side, was also kind to Mary supplying her with bags of rice as gifts. In return, when she was in that area, Mary helped with the sick and was also able to hold services.

Still progress was slow; the natives were reluctant to abandon their bad old ways. Often Mary was in physical danger. It was sometimes a case of one step forwards and two backwards, but she never lost her love of the people and the belief in her call from God. Sometimes she prevailed and sometimes she failed.

'O God, open the eyes of these people,' she prayed, 'I do so want them to leave their evil ways and come to love you.' *'Because of the Lord's great love we are not consumed, for His compassions never fail. They are new every morning; great is Your faithfulness.' (Lamentations 3:22-23.)*

Mary decided to move more permanently to Ekenge and centre her work there. She took five of her little children with her. On the journey she had the company of a missionary printer, Mr Bishop. The journey took five hours and the five bairns were carried either by Mr Bishop, Mary or two of the porters who also had to carry the luggage. When they arrived they found Ekenge deserted except for two guards.

'Where is everyone?' Mary asked.

'Everyone is at Ifako. The mother of their chief has died.'

Mary had a little time to settle herself into her new home. She swept out the hut as much as she could but still had to sleep on the ground like the natives did, along with all the vermin. She hung a curtain over the door, patched the holes in the walls with mud and erected a fence to separate the hut from the livestock. The natives wondered at the bother she was taking.

One time a youth who had been accused of infidelity was to have boiling oil poured over his hands. This was the usual form of punishment for this crime. It was reckoned by the law of the jungle that if he was guilty he would suffer; if innocent, he would feel no pain.

Mary rushed to intervene but she was too late. As the youth was forced to hold out his chained hands the ladle of the boiling oil was poured over them. The young lad screamed and rolled on the ground in agony.

'You silly men! That would be agonizing for *anyone*, whether they were innocent or not! Let's try pouring it over *your* hands.' Mary rushed forward to try to grab the ladle as the tormenter scurried away in fear. Mary was pleased to see the other men jeered and laughed at him.

In all her dealings with the natives she continued to find Eme a great help. Their friendship continued. Mary found her to be extremely intelligent and had many long conversations with her.

Another day a slave was accused, probably falsely, of using witchcraft and condemned to die. Again Mary tried to intervene but the crowd screamed and bayed for his blood. Eventually she prevailed and the chief agreed to lessen his sentence. They agreed that he should just be bound with heavy chains, starved and then flogged. He was beaten within an inch of his life and as he lay, a mass of bleeding flesh, she wondered if she'd actually helped him; death might have been preferable.

A neighbouring chief lay dying. It was requested that Mary should go to heal him. She was in a quandary. If he should die, as was most likely, she would be blamed and probably killed as well. But as a Christian she couldn't ignore the plea for help, as she realised that if he died, many others would be put to death as a sacrifice. After much anguished prayer she went.

The tough journey involved eight hours of battling her way through the sodden jungle. The wild animals again threatened her life, the undergrowth tried to trip her up and she found it necessary to murmur constant prayer as she went. As fear gripped her heart she wondered if she would be making the homeward journey, or would her life end here alone and away from any other missionaries in the jungle?

She arrived to find the men ready for the massacre and the sound of wailing women awaiting their fate. Although wet, cold and feverish, she went straight into the hut and began ministering to the sick man. After many long and fretful days the chief slowly began to recover. Once again God had intervened and many lives were saved that day. Thankfully Mary was able to make the homeward journey.

Then her own Chief Edem became ill and unknown to her sent for the witch doctor. The witch doctor made out to believe that an enemy had put many strange items under the body—cartridges, powder, teeth, bones, eggshells and seeds. Punishment would have to be meted out. Then Mary witnessed a number of men and women being seized, chained to posts and condemned to die.

She then became the 'tigress' that frightened all her opponents and was such a nuisance badgering to set these people free that eventually Chief Edem was secreted away to another village where he was able to recover in peace. Only then were the prisoners released and just one woman died as a result of this witch doctor's wicked plan.

A cruel chief from another village, whom Mary knew and feared, came into her compound, extremely drunk, and with his drunken followers causing uproar and terror.

'We will kill every last person in this village,' they declared.

There seemed to be no stopping them as they crazed around until Mary went and stood right in the very midst of them, refusing to let them pass, although they snarled and snapped at her. As a foreign white woman they didn't dare touch her and she was eventually able to persuade them to return from where they had come.

Nevertheless, the next day they returned and captured one young man who they accused of witchcraft. This time the recovered Chief Edem intervened on Mary's behalf and the young man was released home. Tragedy was averted and peace restored—until the next time.

Tales of cruelty were numerous. A number of wives, some nursing babies, were to be punished for some crime which was unknown to Mary but before the sentence could be carried out the women were left chained all day under the intense blaze of the sun without food or drink. The punishment would take place in the evening. At the one time when they were left unguarded Mary with some of the other women was able to sneak food to them and water which at least kept them alive. If they had been caught they would have been put to death themselves, possibly Mary along with them. Eventually these frightened souls were released unpunished.

One time a girl from the Ebo (Ibo) tribe, noted for her beauty and fine looks, used these to entice a male slave. He was condemned to die for his offence although he had only been the victim of her advances. It was said he'd used sorcery to trap her but Mary required evidence.

'A court of law cannot condemn a man without evidence,' Mary reasoned.

'No evidence is required!' shouted the chief. As the argument went back and forwards, Mary later reported that 'things got critical'. No doubt an understatement! By then the girl in question had committed suicide and the chief lost a valuable commodity. Still Mary wouldn't back down and eventually the man's death sentence was reduced to three days continuous beatings. His final condition was so bad that again Mary thought it might have been better if he'd been executed. Not all her interventions met with success.

Wherever Mary lived her homes seemed to be temporary, but she longed to have somewhere of her own, somewhere to be able to read her Bible and pray in peace away from the overcrowding and squabbling of the others. Knowing that if she wanted something built she would have to do it herself, she set to work. First she fixed stout tree-trunks in the ground and on top of these criss-cross-wise she laid the other pieces. Sticks were then placed between the uprights and strips of bamboo, beaten until soft, were fastened in and out. The work reminded her of the weaving back in Dundee and her heart again ached for her dead family.

The walls were then made by throwing large lumps of clay between the sticks which were rubbed to make a smooth surface. Mats of palm leaves were laid on the top and tied down to form the roof. The furniture she also made out of clay, which was beaten hard, polished and darkened by a native dye.

Then Mary, still plagued by insects, snakes and other animals, dreamed of a house with an upper storey where she would be living with less wild life. But first there was a church to build. Helped by the chief and free men and women, a long roomy shed was built, complete except for windows and doors. Mary then had to teach the people that a church should be regarded with reverence as God's house.

Mary worked in many of the tiny villages often rushing from one to the other to take a service or attend to the sick. She became involved in work both in the villages of Ifako and Ekenge. In the mornings she dispensed medicines and treated ailments and in the afternoons she had 'book' where Edem's wives were all free to attend watched over by Edem and Eme Ete. Although the two villages were only a short distance apart Mary always had to travel with an armed guard.

When Mary first went to Ifako the place was full of drunken and dirty men. Mary complained that the chief there stank but to no avail. Cleanliness was not on their agenda. One thing they were surprised about was that as she trudged through the deep vegetation of the jungle she had an armed guard but no actual fighting men. This Scottish lassie, who in Dundee was afraid of dogs, travelled with boldness through the jungle.

'I've come to teach your people the Word,' she said. 'I will also teach you to keep yourselves clean, how to cook and to care for your babies as well. You will learn 'book' and become traders so that your town will become rich. The people of Ekenge have promised a house for me and ground for the building of a school.'

Not to be outdone, the Ifako chief said, 'We too will give you land and build you a house. We want to learn 'book' and become rich traders.'

'But you must stick to my rules,' Mary said. 'No more punishment without trial and slaves must be treated properly.'

Then she went back to Ekenge, but soon had to pack to go back to Ifako. The wait for a church and two-storey house for herself proved to be a long one.

To get her message across, Mary needed to understand the local customs. These were long established and not easily changed. The people were willing to accept the concept of her god, so long as it was alongside their existing gods. They too believed in overall, all-powerful gods; it was just that they had so many of them.

One battle which Mary had to fight was when a certain slave had done a job for a woman's husband and he continued to demand payment although the husband was away. Eventually borne down by his threats the woman gave him half a yam just to get rid of him. But there was the moral code which said that giving food to another man in the husband's absence was considered a prelude to adultery. The punishment was death.

Mary heard the woman's screams as she was staked out ready for the killing with all the drunk, masked and painted Egbo lusting for her blood. Mary did the only thing she could—she placed herself between the executioner and the intended victim. He swung his ladle of boiling oil nearer and

59

nearer to the writhing figure, intending to burn her to death. Mary was standing in the way. This was a replay of the attack with the leaded weight back in Dundee so many years before. Again Mary won through. The man backed down, the life was saved and Mary went to bed that night giving thanks that on this occasion with the help of God she had succeeded. The people thought it must be evidence that Mary's god was so strong that she could put herself in such danger.

On one occasion when a man had been running amok with a drawn sword, she tripped him up from behind and got the sword from his grasp. Obviously he wasn't expecting her to be so quick on her feet.

Chapter 7

SUCCESSES AND SUPERSTITIONS

NO SOONER had Mary dealt with one emergency than another seemed to occur. Etim, a chief's son, was working in the forest harvesting trees and was struck down by a log he'd been handling. His injuries meant he was very near to death.

'Quick. Come quickly, Ma. Etim is dying.'

Mary got to the injured man and with help carried him to her hut. She nursed him faithfully, but she was fighting a losing battle. In spite of her care, he died. Now she realised that the death of a chief's son at a relatively young age was very bad news. Witchcraft would be blamed and many lives would be lost. Predictably the witchdoctor was sent for. He decided that the death was the fault of the villagers near to the spot where the accident had happened. Mary had the feeling that this could be a turning point in her ministry; she must make good sense prevail but it was going to prove a particularly long battle of wits to prevent the anticipated bloodshed.

Anyone in the accused village who could be found, men, women and children, were rounded up, tied with chains and brought into the Ekenge yard. Tethered to posts, they were expecting their heads to be cut off at any moment.

One very harrowing scene was of a young girl, about fifteen, who ran from person to person crying: 'I'll be a slave for the rest of my life if only you set my mother free!'

At this time Mary was working with another missionary, Mr Ovens, who in the coming years was to feature large in Mary's life and work. He was able to watch over the prisoners both day and night. At first the natives were too drunk to deal with the unfortunate captives. Then Mary saw some little brown beans lying on the ground. These were the beans which were given to anyone accused of a crime to prove their innocence or otherwise. These dreaded poisonous beans were crushed and given to the prisoners to drink. In nearly every case they proved to be fatal.

Mary stormed up to the chief.

'You mustn't let this wicked thing happen!' she raged.

'Leave us alone. What does it matter to you? Your God will not let them die if they are innocent.'

Mary knew there was no arguing with that reasoning but she also knew that without help many innocent people would be killed.

'I will not leave here until all the prisoners are free,' Mary threatened.

Night came. Mary saw two men drag one woman away and just managed to intervene before the poison was drunk. In the confusion and with Mary's intervention the woman managed to escape. Mary ran back to the yard. With Mr Ovens on guard the other prisoners were still safe but the stand-off continued through many weary days and nights.

'We'll set some of the prisoners free and see if that will satisfy Ma,' the witch doctor declared.

Mary was not satisfied, she intended everyone to be safe.

'We'll burn down your house and yard.'

'That's all right. They're not mine anyway.'

Soon only three prisoners were left, the others having been released. Then just one man and woman remained. The man was set free. The woman was doomed to die at nightfall. It seemed Mary could do nothing to save her. But another could.

Under the cover of darkness, Eme Ete stole up to the prisoner, cut the chains that bound her to the post and with her leg-irons still on, the woman crawled to the sanctuary of Ma's hut.

So the funeral of the chief's son took place; there was no human sacrifice—the only sacrifice was a cow. It was the first royal funeral that had taken place in that region with no human blood being shed.

But all did not finish well. At the funeral party two men quarrelled and a man's head was cut off. This meant war was declared resulting in more bloodshed. Revenge followed revenge, bloodshed followed bloodshed. If seemed there were many repercussions. The love of strong liquor and killing was not going to go away easily.

One night Mary heard drums and realised there was mischief afoot. Men and women, half-naked, very drunk and brandishing weapons, rushed into the compound. As they were howling war songs Mary knew they were intent on destruction.

'Give us gin or we make trouble!' they howled as they rushed around. 'We will burn down your village; we will capture your young men.'

'Go and hide in your hut,' Mary was advised.

One particular young woman, seeing that Mary was a white woman, thought she must be rich and yelled even louder to be given gin. Edem and Eme Ete would not let Mary approach her. Full grown warriors she might be able to overcome, but this woman was even more dangerous. Against her will Mary was forced to hide in the hut all night and even in the morning there was still danger.

In her determination Mary eventually overruled them. 'Let them in,' she demanded. She then proceeded to give the drunken woman warrior a lecture on how she should sober up, go home, wash and present herself nicely and care for her husband. Only God could have kept Mary safe at that time. The woman threatened to return but nothing more was heard from her. It is unlikely she took heed of Mary's words but at least this wee missionary was safe for the time being.

Every day she went about her business of teaching and educating the people. She taught by pinning an alphabet card up on a post and had numbers penned on sheets of paper. She sang them songs which they could repeat and then followed this up with prayers where they could all join in. During the day she taught by the light of the tropical sun; by evening she used the glow of lanterns with myriad insects buzzing round the light.

The beauty and rawness of Africa fascinated Mary. She sometimes wrote poetry, the rhymes seeming to best express her emotions:

> *The shimmering, dancing wavelets and the stately solemn palms,*
> *The wild weird chant of the boatmen and the natives' evening psalms,*
> *The noise of myriad insects and the firefly's soft bright sheen,*
> *The bush with its thousand terrors and its never fading green.*

News of her various doings spread and chiefs from further and further afield came to seek her help even if they didn't always take her advice. Although they travelled with weapons, Mary insisted they were all left outside the compound. She baffled them; a slight white lady who was not afraid of full grown warriors was beyond their comprehension. They decided she must have a very powerful god. That was exactly what Mary wanted them to believe—because she knew it was true that God was keeping her safe.

Mary was a Christian who had joy, in spite of her occasional temper which she usually kept it in check. Remembering that

Africa was known as the White Man's grave, life was difficult for her physically. She was often alone and missing Christian stimulation. It was most likely that she sang as she worked and ministered to the people's needs. The fact that she played the organ and sometimes a concertina at the services proved she was musical and therefore it was most natural that her joy should be expressed in song. Her voice, which probably weakened with advancing years, would often be heard joining in with the birdsong and penetrating the lush green jungle.

Another chief lay dying, another challenge for Mary and her God. This was happening in a town some twenty-five miles north of the Cross River, a most dangerous part of the Okoyong. The villagers were already collecting and preparing the Calabar bean ready for a full-scale slaughter.

'I'll go and see what I can do,' Mary declared. She was urged not to go as it was too dangerous but she would not be dissuaded.

'If he dies, they will kill you too,' her friends warned.

Mary nearly hesitated. She was needed here at Ekenge. But she handed the problem to God and set out with an armed guard. Ma Ete was to look after her children while she was gone. Again Mary hoped she would be returning to them. Twenty-five jungle miles was a long and dangerous journey plus the opposition she would encounter when she arrived.

One of her women carried the first aid medicine kit, another head-loaded the food, while the third carried the cooking pot. The going was hard. First Mary discarded her boots which were disintegrating as she walked; then her heavy skirt had to go, then her chemise. In the torrential rain with sodden clothing, Mary was again showing signs of fever but she continued. Half drowned in the knee-deep mire and soaked to the skin, she battled on. Nothing and no-one was going to stop this 'half-naked' woman.

The chief had been in a coma for many days and there was every likelihood Mary would not be able to save his life. She persevered, forcing quinine down his throat, rubbing him with alcohol and laying wet clothes over him to bring down his temperature. It was not enough—she needed more medicine. She knew it would take sixteen hours to get this from Ekenge, but she also knew there was a dispensary over the Cross River at Okorofiong. She asked the men in her party.

'Take this paper to Mr Cruikshank at the dispensary and he will give you the medicine.'

'No, we're afraid. No man is fit to cross the river. Devils live in the river.'

'I'll go myself then.'

Still sick with fever, she stumbled back onto the forest path and after a further two hours reached the river. There she was able to give the note to the boatman.

'I am white Ma from Ekenge. I am a friend of King Eyo.' She used all the influence she could muster to get the man to take the note. Then she waited for his return and much later trudged back through the forest with the life-giving medicine. On her return she gave this to the young chief and then collapsed herself. When she came to, the sick man had recovered, demanding food, and the relieved wives were doing a delighted dance that their lives had been saved. Mary's recovery took longer.

From time to time Mary was joined in her work by other missionaries. One such was Charles Morrison, a quiet young man not long out from Scotland. Being a fellow Scot, he and Mary soon became good friends. They related well to each other as they both had periods of home-sickness. Although he was seventeen years younger than Mary there was a great deal about him that Mary liked.

When Mary was visiting Duke Town, where he was working, he brought her books to read and flowers from the mission compound. These kindnesses made Mary's life easier. He loved to hear her speak about life in the Okoyong and shared with her that he had a desire to become a writer. He often showed her his work which she praised and admired.

Eventually he was able to travel out to Ekenge and see with his own eyes the work she was accomplishing. They grew closer over time and it was not surprising given the circumstances that they began to fall in love. The age difference didn't cause a problem to them but Mary realised that he was not very strong physically and the extreme climate was beginning to take a toll on his health. Before long Charles asked Mary to marry him.

She prayed long and hard about this proposal. There was no doubt that she was in love with him and she longed to have someone to share in her work. But above all she knew she must do God's will.

'My life is here in the Okoyong. That is my priority,' she told him.

'If the board don't let me come to Okoyong you must come back here to Duke Town,' he said.

'No, I couldn't leave my people.'

They both needed to exercise patience and seek God's will.

The work continued. Mary eventually was able to shame Chief Edem into building her a new house at Ifako after she had threatened to build it herself. It was right next to his harem house which at times could be embarrassing. The two-roomed house was made of mud and wattle with a roof of palm leaves extended over the front to make a veranda. There were storerooms at either end. The living room had clay bunks which could be used if necessary; the other room was where Mary slept, often accompanied by a number of small children. She also managed to squeeze in her portable organ, sewing machine and her beloved books.

Then work started on the church. It was twenty-five foot by thirty foot, also made of mud and wattle and intended to double up as a school. Everyone was involved in the building work; the women smoothed the floors and fashioned and polished the clay benches for the pews. Mary requested that no slave should be involved in the work, only free women who were doing the work from choice.

For the first service everyone wanted to dress in their best clothes. Fortunately the occasion coincided with the arrival of a box of clothes sent from Scotland. Mary reflected on the sacrifice of the donors and was very grateful for these regular boxes of clothes and gifts. For the occasion those who wished could wear the donated clothes while others were able to 'wear their own skin' if they wished.

'I wish there was someone to fit the windows and doors. The natives don't know how to do that and nor do I.'

Help was at hand. Charles Ovens, another Scotsman and a carpenter, had arrived armed with all the necessary skills. The building work was soon finished. Mary had realised that when the natives were busy working they had less time to drink. She knew that to keep them employed was one way of lessening the bad effects of liquor.

She tried to get the traders from Calabar to visit Okoyong, but they were frightened as they were often attacked when they tried to trade their wares. Mary wrote to King Eyo Honesty requesting that the chiefs of Okoyong visit Creek Town to discuss trade between the two areas.

With her usual persistence she managed to arrange a palaver, a meeting where both sides could meet to discuss the problem. A further difficulty appeared when Mary wouldn't let the natives travel in the canoes with their weapons. This was complete madness to them. No Okoyong person would travel without his spear, dagger, machete or gun. As they sailed down the river Mary noticed weapons hidden in the canoes. With no thought for her own safety, one by one she hurled the offensive weapons overboard into the river, nearly decapitating some of the warriors in her fervour. Her 'carrots' temperament, never far below the surface, had erupted again.

The memorable meeting started. King Eyo Honesty VII dazzled the Okoyong chiefs with all his possessions. The thought behind this opulence was that if they could make this trade idea work, both sides could have such riches. King Eyo sat at the head of the proceedings wearing a shiny black top hat decorated with parrot feathers. In his hand he held a sceptre of finest polished silver.

Mary started the palaver by washing her hands from a basin of water and then all the guests had their hands washed. The banquet followed and what a banquet it was—yams stuffed with peppers, black soup, manioc and fish soup, fried plantains, cocoyams, bananas, corn, roast goat, chicken, beef, fish and sweets! Even Mary was surprised at the opulence of the meal.

This sumptuous repast was followed by a service. Then the king explained that the entire coast was now protected by the British and the British would see that the trade in palm oil would not be disrupted in any way. Not only would trade be encouraged but armed soldiers would be sent into the jungle to arrest people who practised the terrible old way of twin murders and human sacrifice.

The chiefs were amazed at the esteem with which Mary was regarded by King Eyo as well as throughout the whole of Creek Town. To show their appreciation they decided to extend Mary's existing two-roomed abode at Ekenge into a building to rival any building in Calabar. They wanted it known that they held the same regard for Mary. She was astonished that the very next Monday, contrary to African speed, work commenced on her house. Usually matters didn't happen so quickly in Africa. But now their pride in her was working to her advantage. No longer did she have to endure the hardship of a small mud hut where her belongings had to be put outside each night so that there would be room for her and her babies to sleep.

Things began to change. The chiefs started to visit Creek Town on a regular basis as there was now a ready market for their palm oil for which a good rate of exchange had been negotiated. The work meant that there was less drinking with the inevitable problems it led to. The children who were sent to school made good progress and the church was well attended. The only sadness for Mary was that there seemed to be a lack of true conversions. The people were enthusiastic as they sang songs to the accompaniment of Mary's playing, but there was little depth to what they sang. But Mary knew she could only sow the seed and had to leave the results to God.

Chapter 8

FRIENDS AND FAILURES

OVER THE YEARS various other missionaries joined Mary in her work. Miss Young, Margaret and Elizabeth were young women from Scotland, who having heard Mary speak about her work, volunteered and for a number of years served God faithfully in the Dark Continent.

The story of how Charles Ovens came to Calabar is particularly interesting. In England he had been ready to sail to America and had already bought his tickets. In March 1889 he read in the *Missionary Record* that Mary Slessor in Calabar was looking for a carpenter to assist in various building works. He knew he had the expertise and was so impressed by what he read that he immediately changed his ticket and volunteered to travel to Africa. Always having wanted to be a missionary he now felt that this was God's call to him. Charles had a sense of adventure as he applied for the position though he had little idea of what lay in store for him. He and Mary got on very well straight away, sharing the same sense of humour and his fine tenor voice always stirred her heart. But even that had a downside. One native remarked, 'I don't like his singing. It makes my heart big and my eyes water.'

When Ovens arrived one of his first jobs was to complete the church at Ifako which still had no windows or doors. Even so the building was the pride of the area. The result of his work was that a building fever started as buildings started to spring up everywhere and Charles was kept well employed.

After a number of years when most of the building work was completed, Ovens was almost finished himself. The fierce sun and high temperatures had taken their toll of his health. Mary nursed him faithfully until he was strong enough to return to Duke Town and then back to Scotland. The natives were not the only ones to miss him. Mary missed his cheerful laughter and the boom of his fine tenor voice in the evening hymns.

Like the characters in the Bible, Christian friends had always been important to Mary; Rev Logie, Mr Thompson, Charles Morrison and now Charles Ovens, all featured largely in her Christian life.

By late 1890 Mary's leave was well overdue but it was difficult to find a replacement. Now she often had a fever and was seldom completely fit. Eventually Margaret Dunlop volunteered to take her place while she took a much needed rest. Edem and Eme gave assurances that they would keep an eye on things while Mary went back to Britain to recover. It is recorded that when Mary did eventually return to Calabar Miss Dunlop was only too pleased to leave as she had found the work very difficult—more difficult than she had expected.

With her replacement settled in it still wasn't easy for Mary to get away. Yet another problem arose. News came through that a battle was taking place many miles away and Mary's assistance was needed. She responded, although her leaving time was drawing near. Edem insisted on sending an escort with her as well as a drummer to ensure her safety. On arriving at the place of the uprising Mary spotted that the chief was someone she had met over a year before and was able to appeal to him for help. With his backing she was able to call a palaver and a resolution to the problem was found.

There was still a further difficulty. The payment settlement of the dispute was to be made in gin. Mary knew this would cause further problems. Now she was able to use her knowledge of the local customs to her advantage. She didn't want the gin drunk all at once which would cause more drunkenness and further fighting. She threw her outer garment over the crate knowing that according to local custom the people wouldn't be able to touch it. She was then able to dole out the gin in small measures, lessening the effect of the drunkenness. The warring men were then happy to return home. Another problem had been resolved.

With this extra excursion Mary was in a further state of collapse but with help she managed to return to Duke Town where her belongings were packed and the party ready to set off. Janie and Little Mary would be travelling with her; her other children would be cared for in Duke Town mainly by Miss Dunlop.

On this occasion she travelled with a secret. Packed in her luggage was her new engagement ring. She had agreed to marry Charles Morrison. Also in her luggage were two books, one written by him, and inscribed in her suitor's hand. She had a photograph taken wearing her engagement ring and until the day she died she always kept by her bedside the two books, *Eugene Aram,* and Charles's copy of *Sketches by Boz*, written by Charles Dickens. But on the whole they tried to keep their engagement a secret until their future was decided.

It is thought that at this time Mary did something which she had never done before. Still being in doubt about her future with Charles, she opened her Bible at a random place. It was Exodus 20:5: *'For I, the Lord thy God, am a jealous God.'* She then felt guilty and closed her Bible but she took this as a sign that she was not to continue her romance. However, the decision was taken out of the couple's hands. The Mission Board decided that Charles was too valuable an asset to be sent out to Ekenge. He was not allowed to go and had to stay in Duke Town. Mission Boards at that time were not too willing for their single missionaries to marry, so Mary's romance, now that it was discovered, was not very popular. One way and another, there was to be no continuance of their romance. Mary knew she could never leave her charges in the jungle; she realised she loved God more than she loved Charles Morrison.

Meanwhile Charles, whose health deteriorated, was invalided back to England while Mary continued her work in Calabar. He was sent to the drier climate of North Carolina for his failing health. There he lived in a log cabin and tried to compensate for his loss by writing. He took the break-up very badly. Not only that but a disastrous fire destroyed much of his work and belongings. He became discouraged and hopeless and was not to live very long. After his death, Mary, who had visited his mother in Kirkintilloch, sent a letter of condolence in which she revealed the depth of her feelings for the old woman's son.

Her colleagues were wise enough not to broach the subject and outwardly Mary put the incident behind her, but to her dying day she never forgot him.

January 1891 saw Mary with Little Mary and Janie sailing into Plymouth. Her first port of call was the Topsham cemetery in Devon where her sister and mother had been buried a number of years before. She was also able to visit and thank the kind folk who had cared for her family when she had decided to go back to Africa. An attack of influenza and bronchitis delayed her return to Scotland, but once she felt stronger the three of them were able to travel north. Above all there was sadness; she still missed her own family.

With regained strength she continued up to Scotland to stay with her old friend Mrs McCrindle in Joppa. Deputation meetings followed. Mary still dreaded speaking at these meetings, especially as for a number of years she had spoken little English. Now she only thought in the African language, Efik.

Back in Glasgow one night Mary found Janie scrubbing the soles of her feet with great vigour. These were the palest parts of her body and when asked what she was doing, Janie replied, 'My feet are getting whiter. If I rub hard maybe I'll become white all over.' Mary felt this was so sad. Janie should have been proud of her darker skin.

One of the things which Mary hoped to accomplish while she was in Scotland was to find someone who was interested in raising money to build a boys' home in Calabar. She was looking for someone to sponsor the scheme and help her to bring it to fruition. The boys back in Calabar needed to learn to be skilful with their hands as well as using their brains. Then maybe Calabar could have a more competent workforce and increase its prosperity, she reasoned.

Her good idea was eventually taken on and it was in 1895 that the school, now known as the Hope Waddell Training Institution, was founded. The Rev Hugh Masterton Waddell had commenced working with friendly slaves in Calabar in 1846 and this institution named after him accomplished much for the evangelism of the west coast of Africa. He lived long enough to see the institution up and running.

At first the building was a prefabricated classroom block of corrugated iron sheets which was built in Glasgow and then shipped to Africa where it was assembled. Between 1900 and 1942 students were enrolled from all over West Africa. Today it is operated with a grammar school curriculum. Over the years thousands of young men were trained there and were enabled to grow up and help their country.

February 1892 saw Mary return to Africa and continue to teach the people. Until they learned to read and write themselves they always wondered about the black marking on a white cloth, which seemed to have a special significance to Mary. This writing which she could do was thought to be some kind of illusion, an idea which Mary fostered until they could read and write for themselves.

In 1900 the British Protectorates of Northern and Southern Nigeria had come into existence and Sir Ralph Moor became responsible for the Southern Nigeria region. He discovered that the slave-trade, cannibalism and exploitation still existed in a larger area and many hundreds of miles hadn't been penetrated by the white man. He attempted to put an end to the slave trade from Arochuku and was forced to take military action. The Aro Expedition was intended to wipe the 'Oracle' off the face of the earth, but it didn't achieve its purpose until December 1901.

All the missionaries, including Mary, had to be evacuated to Duke Town, where Mary hadn't visited for years. She found changes. Once there she was pleased to see that under the guidance of J. K. Macgregor who had become principal of the Hope Waddell Training Institute, it had continued to function along the lines she had suggested in the first place. On their first meeting Mr Macgregor had described Mary as 'a slim figure of middle height with fine eyes full of power'. He added: 'It is wonderful to sit and listen to her talking, for she is most fascinating and besides being a humourist is a fine source of information on mission history and Efik customs.'

One of the African ways to solve problems was to have a palaver. These were meetings where both sides of a point of view met to discuss the matter. Often these were long drawn out affairs which could last for many days. Mary was able to make use of these meetings to solve problems and it was often she who decided to call them. While knitting to keep both her mind and hands busy, she would follow all sides of the arguments very carefully. The knitting meant that whatever the outcome the time wasn't wasted and something tangible and useful came out of it all. She also indulged in her love of tea and biscuits while she listened.

One Sunday when Mary was resting between her services she heard a great commotion. Four Egbo runners were slashing at a slave woman. The woman was dragged into a neighbouring hut while they continued to beat and slash her half naked body. Mary fearlessly rushed into the hut and grabbed the whip from one of the attackers.

'How dare you break the Sabbath in my town!' she cried, almost as upset at the Sunday intrusion as the poor whipped slave.

The Egbo shouted back at her: 'You no savvy Egbo fashion! Egbo master of all people. How you drive Egbo man!'

'Sit down and talk about it!' Mary ordered.

It seemed the woman was a widow and she was being held responsible for her late husband's debts. For years she and her husband had paid instalments and interest off a debt but now he had died. The Egbo men still demanded their money in this barbaric way. Mary insisted that they leave and that the widow paid no more money to them. She knew that the Egbo were just trying to prove their power but Mary had a power of her own.

'Go and don't come back unless you come in peace.' Such was her authority that they obeyed.

On another day the Aros stole one of Eme's slaves. Their intention was to kill her then sell her as meat in Eastern Nigeria. Unfortunately this was a common practice. Rushing over to Eme's place, Mary found the villagers armed with guns, spears and machetes, trying to outwit the gang. Altogether there were four slaves, chained down and terrified. Mary noted that the Aros were very drunk but this didn't stop her. She stood between the warring forces. The Aros people were taken aback; they'd heard about this mad white woman but these particular men hadn't seen her before.

'Take the chains off these slaves,' she demanded. 'They're our slaves.'

It took many hours before Mary got her way and the Aros slunk away. Peace reigned for a short time but there always seemed to be a new emergency for her to deal with.

Mary was ill again; her leave was almost a year overdue. Her furlough was arranged and at her own expense she took her four girls back to Scotland with her; Janie sixteen, Little Mary five, Alice three and Maggie sixteen months. With little warning they arrived to stay with a friend in Portobello where Little Mary attended school for a short time. The children were also allowed to paddle in the sea—a great novelty for them. Then they all moved down to Bowden St Boswells. Mary had to give the usual round of lectures and talks. Their journey to Britain this time had been via Liverpool, both there and back, and while they were away from Africa Charles Ovens took over the work.

On a Sunday, which was to be remembered by the Scottish worshippers for a long time, the people were noisy while a collection was being taken up. This was not to Mary's liking. 'Don't you know these offerings are for the Lord?' she called out. 'Is this not an act of worship? Then where is your reverence? The most impoverished convert in Calabar would not be so thoughtless as to chatter during worship and when the collection is being taken up.' Mary still had her fiery temper and outspoken ways. Their stay was a short one. In less than a year they were back in Africa.

In August 1903 Mary had been serving on the mission field in Africa for twenty-seven years. An ordained missionary was sent out to work with her and was able to administer the Sacraments of Baptism and the Lord's Supper. Mary was now beginning to feel that after many years of hard work, results were taking place.

Mary had described the Ibibios at Itu as 'untamed, unwashed and unlovely savages', but in 1903 she was able to start a mission there. In due course there would be a church, Sunday School, day school and medical base. Janie and Mary settled there a year later. Under their guidance and the power of the Lord the area was beginning to change greatly.

As Mary became older she was not capable of rushing around as she had in the past. Gone were the days when she would run a few miles to administer help. One form of transport suggested to her was to use a bicycle. The problem was that this fearless pioneer was afraid of bicycles. She thought they would explode. But when one was sent out as a gift from England, in gratitude she had to learn to ride it and it proved to be a great help to her.

A number of good things then happened. The Church of Scotland allowed her to make Itu a regular station with a doctor in charge of the medical centre. The hospital which was eventually built was called the Mary Slessor Mission Hospital. This still exists today and continues to care for the sick and dying. A launch sent out from England further helped work up and down the Creek and another mission station was set up at Arochuku.

The skill Mary had with the natives did not go unnoticed. She was appointed as a Vice-consul and asked to act as judge between the warring factions of the Aros and Ibo and to sort out problems up the Enyong River. Such was the faith in her that her decisions were respected.

She was asked to be a magistrate as she understood so well the native customs. Her initial reply was, 'I don't want to do it but for His sake I will.'

Mary was getting older and about this time started to suffer with arthritis. This wasn't surprising in view of her age and the dampness of the climate, although she did reckon that it was aggravated by the type of house that Charles Ovens had built for her. He would have been wiser to follow the native design which took into account the extreme damp weather conditions.

Chapter 9

MARY'S SECRET WEAPON

It has been said that whenever we breathe a thought to God we are praying which means that God is only a breath away. Mary had more to say and write about prayer than any other subject. She would never have achieved all that she did without being in constant communication with her Master. Prayer was what she practised and was the frequent subject in her diaries and in her letters home.

Many of her quotations have been amalgamated into a calendar compiled by Mrs W. A. Livingstone which has proved to be much used by Mary's followers. January 10th gives her quote: *'Pray in a businesslike fashion, earnestly, definitely, steadily.'* It is easy to imagine Mary having put her young charges to sleep, settling down under the African sky to spend a few moments or even longer with the creator of the earth and the author of her much-loved Bible. As she read her Bible it became full of numerous marginal notes, so that she would often have to commence writing on another Bible.

February 5th suggests, *'If only we prayed and had more faith, what a difference it would make.'* Maybe Mary's faith did sometimes waver when faced with almost insurmountable odds. This would have driven her to her knees to pray even more earnestly.

Her followers must have felt her near as they read on June 30th, *'God has been good in letting me serve Him in this humble way. I can't thank Him enough for the honour He has conferred on me when He sent me to a dark continent.'* What an attitude to have in view of all the dangers she was constantly facing! Her thoughts were only of thankfulness, never self-pity.

Mary believed that prayer could take place at anytime and anywhere. In the dangers she had to face in the jungle, she often prayed 'arrow prayers'. There was no time to be formal; no time for a 'Dear Lord', or 'Amen'. She had to appeal for help immediately. A drunken warrior or dying baby would not wait while she made an elaborate request. Extended prayer was kept for morning and evening devotions, but Mary would have found it necessary to offer up these arrow prayers at all parts of the day. *'Make a habit of praying while looking up and saying a word or two in thought at any time,'* was what she once wrote. It's easy to think of Mary doing just this as she faced an African rampaging mob or when she sighted an alligator in the fast flowing rivers. She considered that praying and keeping in touch with God was all powerful and wanted others to follow her example.

'Prayer can do anything. Let's try its power.' This was not something she wanted to keep to herself; others could be in possession of this power. It was only prayer that could defeat the power of the witch doctors and their charms.

'Don't stop praying.' As said in the Bible, Mary wanted her praying to be continuous. It was a reminder to herself as well as to others to be steadfast in prayer.

'Jacob's ladder has never been withdrawn; it has been the highway for help all through the years.' This was a beautiful and picturesque thought. Mary knew that the God of the Old Testament was also her God. His power was still as strong.

'Prayer is the greatest power God has put into our hand for service. Prayer is harder work than doing... but the dynamic that way is to advance the kingdom... pray that the prayer may

rest upon me, that He may never be disappointed, or find me disobedient to the heavenly vision when He shows the way.'

Prayer was no easy option for her. It was not an alternative for action; it just came first. Although her prayer life was important, Mary's life was a lot of doing but in the quote above she considers that prayer was more difficult. *'It is easy in our doings to forget to pray. But that would be like running a car with no fuel or doing the washing with no soap.'* Again she was painting a picture in her mind. Prayer was the basic ingredient in Mary's life. She needed to be in constant communication with God.

Quotes came quick and fast,

'If only we prayed and had more faith, what a difference it would make.'

'Once I had to deal with a group of warlike men and I received God's strength to face them because I felt someone was praying for me, just then. If only you are inclined to pray for a missionary, do it at once wherever you are.' Mary always urged that if anyone felt the thought to pray for a missionary they should do it immediately. That prompting could be sent at exactly the right time when the need was there. Missionaries might be out of our sight but their needs continue to be great.

'My life is one long daily, hourly record of answered prayer.' Mary often knew the joy of answered prayer. She didn't only pray to God; she was receiving answers from Him. She had a dialogue with Him as if He was physically with her on this earth.

'Nothing drives a man or a nation to prayer like trouble.' Mary had her share of problems, danger and trouble and believed that an easy life could cause a shift away from God.

It was at her mother's knee that Mary learned to put the Lord first. Mrs Slessor in spite of a difficult life 'took everything to God in prayer.' In having a husband who drank away the money which should have been spent on food for the family, Mrs Slessor was always in a state of poverty. Having her priority in prayer she endeavoured to do God's will and train her children in the same way. Drink was Mr Slessor's answer to problems, prayer was hers.

The Bible warns against being strongly addicted to anything except Himself. *'You shall have no other gods before me.... For I the Lord your God am a jealous God.' (Exodus 20:3&5.)*

Mary put the Lord first in her life. She embraced the hardships of Africa for God; she turned down the offer of marriage so that she could continue to do God's will.

'Love the Lord your God with all your heart and with all your soul and with all your strength.' (Deuteronomy 6:5.)

The love of God should preclude all other loves in our lives which may not in themselves be harmful but bad if taken to excess. Mary applied the rule of 'God first' in all her life. Although she had loved her family and had worked well at the mill, her first love was for the Africans, especially the children. Because of the time she spent with Him in prayer, her love for God deepened.

With the arrival of the British the region began to open up and Mary received more visitors. One welcome visitor was Mary Henrietta Kingsley, anthropologist, naturalist and niece of Charles Kingsley the novelist. At thirty-two years old, Miss Kingsley was as individual a personality as Mary Slessor was herself. She had been a guest of the Consul-General at Duke Town for several months looking for rare specimens of fish and discovering the mysteries of the West African culture. She invited herself to visit Mary and although she was a woman of the world and Mary was a Christian, they recognised in each other kindred spirits. Miss Kingsley later said of her times spent with Mary that they were some of the most pleasant of her life.

Smartly dressed with a velvet torque on her head and high-buttoned boots, she contrasted sharply with the plain clothed missionary. They sat together night after night discussing, arguing and often agreeing on many subjects. Miss Kingsley described Mary as 'a very wonderful lady'. The two women continued to keep up a correspondence until Miss Kingsley's death of enteric fever in 1900 in South Africa while nursing Boer War prisoners.

Mary had yet more to say about prayer:

'Prayer is the greatest power God has put into our hands for service.' Also how near she must have felt to God when she said, *'God never gives vague instructions.'* And she did need to keep close to God when she wrote, *'Christ will never leave the world, though we may leave Him, then the light is gone.'*

On more than one occasion, she said *'God and one are a majority.'* Often she was that one. She used the Bible as a handbook for prayer and a means of supplication. *'Answer me when I call to You, O my righteous God. Give me relief in my distress; be merciful to me and hear my prayer.'* (Psalms 4:1.)

She used prayer as a means of seeking forgiveness: *'Be kind and considerate to one another, forgiving each other, just as in Christ God forgave you.'* (Ephesians 4:32.)

Or: *'Who can forgive sins, but God alone?'* (Mark 2:7.)

Mary found rest and comfort through prayer: *'He makes me to lie down in green pastures. He leads me beside quiet waters.'* (Psalms 23:3.)

Prayer was also a way for Mary to give thanks to God: *'Praise the Lord, oh my soul; all my inmost being, praise His holy name.'* (Psalm 103:1.)

Chapter 10

LETTERS FROM AFRICA

BEING ABLE TO READ the letters which Mary sent back to Britain gives a further and enlightening insight to her character. In 1993 a relative of Miss Crawford, who had been an administrator in the Free Church of Scotland and friend of Mary's, gave copies of Mary's letters to the City of Dundee. A great deal of what we know about Mary today was discovered in these letters.

Since then in 1998 considerable work has been done by Leslie A MacKenzie and Ruth Riding in transcribing Mary's letters as well as articles which were written about her in the then current Christian magazines. These have been put on the Dundee Centre Library website and have kindly been made free of copyright, so long as any quotes are acknowledged to www.DundeeCity.gov.uk/MarySlessor/lettersandarticles

The letters fall into two groups, those to Charles Partridge, District Commissioner in Ikot Okpene in the territory of the Ibibio people (classed as political). Mary's last letter to him was 24th December 1914, so close to her death. Those to Miss Crawford and other Christian friends (classed as ecclesiastical) were always immensely readable and often displayed her sense of humour. Whenever time allowed Mary loved communicating with her friends.

In one letter Mary describes herself as 'wee and thin and not very strong.' Wee and thin she might have been, though some photos would seem to show otherwise, but her stamina and endurance cannot be denied. As the only member among her siblings to survive to a good age she endured the hardships of the African jungle for many years. It was not expected that missionaries to the continent of Africa would survive for many years and when Mary had to return to Scotland for a furlough after a period of only two years it was feared that she would never be strong enough to return. Her love for the work of God, her determination and something of an obviously strong stamina, won her through.

Her workload was always enormous. She said in one letter, *'Once got home to find fifty people needing advice. Took till midnight.'* That would have been no excuse not to start work very early the next morning. *'Oh, if only I were 30 years younger and a man,'* she bemoaned.

An unknown author wrote of Mary's schedule on 16 August 1902: *'Mary Slessor at 6 a.m. goes to a village three miles away to hold a school. Home at ten, always someone wanting a palaver. After school in a house here. After tea attends the sick. Every four days market day when she had a lot of visitors. Sabbath at six a.m. to village where she has the school and holds a service. Then with some boys to a more distant place. Comes home and has two meetings in two different villages. In evening has a service for the children. Great change in the last thirteen years. Husbands would not be with their wives if they had twins, now I see them together.'*

In 1901 Mary was asked for evidence of her date of birth. She replied, *'It was either 1847 or 1848 but the records have been eaten by ants.'* Humidity and ants were a great problem in Calabar for retaining any type of paperwork.

As Mary's fame grew, both at home and in Africa, she was continually being asked to share her story, either by talks when she was in Britain or by articles when she was back in Africa. Her busy schedule allowed little space for this as time spent writing articles would be time away from her numerous tasks.

She wasn't above firmly declining to write these but tried to remain polite as well. During the last few years of her life she was asked for a contribution of some aspect of her work which she declined in a lengthy letter and pointing out the many things that she did do. She described her reply as a *'small friendly letter to show I am not soured or cynical.'*

Extracts of many of Mary's letters or reference to them were reproduced in the *Women's Missionary Magazine* and the *Missionary Recorder,* the magazines which her mother had been so happy to read.

In March 1904 the *Women's Missionary Magazine* stated: *'Miss Slessor, whose furlough now falls due, has chosen to spend it in Old Calabar, rather than return to the homeland. She intended to enter the Inokon country by way of the Itu and the Enyon Creek, with the hope of extending mission operations in that direction.'* No doubt many of her followers were disappointed not to be seeing her in person in Scotland, but this period was what she described as 'her gypsy holiday.'

After having received a large Christmas pudding from Charles Partridge in December 1904 Mary thanked him on 6 January 1905 and said they ate it for breakfast, tea and dinner and then breakfast. As Mary's family was quite extensive at this time, it must have been a very large pudding.

She writes on 17 January 1906, *'The court takes up a great deal of my time but I do not know how to let any of it go, for it holds such possibilities for good.'* In the event she did give it up a few years later.

After Mary had her one and only holiday in the Canary Islands, she wrote to Miss Crawford, *'It was worth waiting a lifetime for, so perfect was it all... Well, it has come to a close in one sense but I am so well, so changed altogether that of course, it is not done and I trust it will be like Elijah's meal in its results.'* She was referring to the widow at Zarephath where Elijah miraculously provided grain until the famine was over in

2 Kings chapter 4. Mary's improved health was in many ways like Elijah's meal, for her strength returned again and again.

In another letter Mary again referred to the Bible. *'If He has promised that we can take up serpents, why should we be afraid of leopards?'*

She much appreciated her friendship with Miss Crawford and on 6 November 1907 wrote to her, *'Dear Daughter of the King, your newly established friendship is one of God's most precious gifts to me on this furlough.'* Living mostly in Africa, her friends in her homeland were few and far between.

The letters clearly show that as other missionaries were commissioned to work in the area, Mary was able to realise her dream to penetrate deeper into the unconquered jungle.

'What is courage but faith conquering fear?' She knew the fear, she had the faith and therefore she had the courage.

In 1912 Mary wrote, *'Early last year I had to go under doctor's orders so more or less had to do things in a soft sort of way which would not let one feel satisfied.'* One can imagine that doing things in a 'soft way' was not to Mary's liking at all.

Mary's letters throw further light into her life and work and although there are in existence very few recordings of Mary's speaking voice, to read Mary's letters is the nearest we can get to hearing her.

Chapter 11

THE HONOURED MISSIONARY

IN THE LAST FEW DECADES of her life, Mary had a further honour bestowed on her. Under the British control the whole area was known as the Niger Coast Protectorate and in 1891 Sir Claude MacDonald was appointed as Consul. Faced with the problem of controlling the area, he knew he didn't have enough knowledge of the natives and their customs. Therefore he turned to the only person he knew who had this knowledge. Because Mary knew the people so well and was revered by them, he asked Mary to be Vice-consul of the Native Court. At that time she was the first woman judge in the British Empire and in this capacity Mary was able to impose sentences of up to six months.

'If I accept, I will not take a salary,' Mary declared.

'But you must, it goes with the job.'

'I will not.'

'This is what we'll do. We'll pay you £1 a year and you can give that to the mission work.' The arrangement seemed acceptable to Mary.

On most days the sessions lasted as long as eight hours and Mary had to sit, listen and weigh up the evidence. Meanwhile she knitted and drank her cups of tea which she loved so much. She also ate biscuits and raided a tin of sweets. But she wasn't just a passive listener. As the natives sometimes behaved like naughty children Mary was quite capable of giving them a slap or rap over the knuckles. Many a chief received a tap on the head by her umbrella. She was once heard to say, 'You have grown so big that you will soon be hitting your head against the roof.'

At times Mary was too ill to attend the court so the court gathered outside her bedroom window and she heard the evidence from there. The oath used in court was not the British one but a native one known as 'mbiam'. A pot or bottle was filled with a secret liquid which had a horrible smell. One of the chiefs would dip the tip of his stick into this and put some of the liquid onto the tongue, head, arm or foot of the witness, who believed that if they told a lie it would kill them.

The time came when this court work was taking up too much of Mary's time and she chose to resign. She was still travelling around saving babies, treating the sick and also choosing to conduct numerous services.

In 1905 instead of taking a furlough Mary was given permission to wander further and further into the jungle, preaching and treating as she went. She did this at her own expense. She argued that by spending her furlough in Africa she was saving the mission society her fare back to Britain. During this period many further tribes and villages were reached. Mary felt encouraged because there had been some conversions, evils had been overcome and villages had become safer places to live.

By April 1906 she had to stop what she described as her 'gypsy style life' and moved her work to Akpap. She was still allowed to remain with the Ibibios which pleased her very much.

Then in May 1906 she was again asked to be a vice-consul; this time to the Ibibios at Ikotobong. Again Mary approached this task with vigour and enthusiasm. The hours were long, the work tiring and Mary's other demands did not lessen. By November 1909 Mary felt again that it was right to resign from this court work. Again it was taking up too much of her time and as her health weakened she was able to do less and less. It was a wrench for her but she needed to remember she wasn't as strong as she had been. She said, 'I shall be sorry to give up the court work as it gives so many opportunities for spreading the gospel.'

Following the idea of Mr Thompson whom she had met on the boat going out to Africa on her first visit to this continent, she planned to build a rest home for missionaries. There was one snag; only Africans could buy land and as a European this was not permitted to her. Never one to be daunted by a piece of legislation, Mary acquired the land in the name of Janie who was of course African. Afraid that the venture might be a failure, the missionary society was not keen for missionary money to be spent on this project, so Mary used her own money. She had a nest egg of a hundred dollars and this was enough to get started. Now Janie, much to her surprise, became a land-owner and the work commenced.

A small piece of ground on the wooded hills nearer the Creek called Use in the Arochuku region was purchased. This had once been the centre of the slave trade. Amazingly most of the work was done by Mary with help from Janie.

But by 1907 all was not well with Mary's health. The extreme climate was beginning to take its toll. She was unable to walk more than a few steps and had to be carried from place to place. The progress of the work was very slow and it was decided that she needed to return to Britain. Mary left Africa in May of that year and this time took Dan, one of her rescued twins, with her, while the work at Akpap was left to Miss Wright.

Back home her plea was, 'Send workers to dark Africa.' She knew she would not be able to carry on her work for much longer and she longed for it to continue among the Africans who so much needed to hear the gospel and be helped in their social improvements. One small matter of interest was that while Mary was in Bonkie, Lanarkshire, she received a gift of a tuning fork from the precentor. This she kept to the end of her days, although towards the end of her life its use would have been limited as her hearing was failing.

At this time, which was to be the last of her furloughs to Scotland, she stayed from May until October. Then she heard some distressing news. Janie was failing in her Christian example and falling into sinful ways. This later proved to be untrue though Mary never did learn who had started this vicious rumour. But she asked if she could return to Africa in the October of 1907. As she sailed back, although she knew her health was failing, she didn't know that she had just had her last visit home. In a few years she planned she would return but she was never able to make another trip.

On her return to Africa Mary found that Miss Wright was not feeling confident to continue working alone at Akpap so Mary spent much of her time travelling between Itu and Akpap. Work was continuing well at Itu where 300 people were attending the church built by themselves, and at the school there were sixty-eight pupils. This church and school had been erected without any financial aid from the mission. But these days Mary was acting more in a supervisory role as her strength lessened; she was very good at giving orders.

Over her time in Africa Mary had built or was responsible for the erection of a number of buildings. There was a school at Amasu and at Arochuku, there was also a school house. Buildings also came into being at Obio, Okpo, Odot and Asang. She was not alone in her efforts; Chief Onoyom at Akani Obio had saved three hundred pounds and built a church for his village.

Mary moved to her recently built home at Use which was near to the new great highway. The area was bordered by giant cotton trees and palms and the road ran up and down over hills and had the advantage of never touching a village or town.

This road was quiet except for market days. Disturbance to the villages had been kept to a minimum during the building but the area was slowly opening up and travelling was becoming easier.

Mary, now old, white-hired and wrinkled, was suffering with rheumatism. Often she was too tired to take her clothes off at night. As much as her health allowed she continued preaching and teaching, training the boys and girls and carrying the light of the gospel. This was her primary work followed by looking after the physical needs of the people. Her largest congregation was to be found at Akani Obio but often she was so ill she had to be carried there.

When Mary made a five-week visit to Duke Town in 1908 she found the town had changed. The trade between the town and the interior had now been established and the region was more prosperous. Another improvement Mary heard about was that some mothers of twins were being accepted back into their families and fewer twin babies were being killed.

In 1911 the area suffered a particularly bad tornado and her house was hit. She still managed to be involved in repairing it. Unfortunately at this time she suffered a mild heart attack and needed to rest, though this was almost impossible for her.

Although many of her building works were finished in her lifetime, such as the Mary Slessor Hospital, the rest home for missionaries and others, some were not finished until after her death. The home for women and girls was one of these as well as the Training Institute and the Wherley Memorial School for Boys.

Mary had discovered the secret of 'peace which the world cannot give'. Peace is often described in negative terms— 'absence of tension', or 'living without hostility'; Saint Augustine of Hippo defined it as 'the tranquillity of order'.

As Mary trudged through the jungle alone facing wild animals, rampaging natives and superstition, she was needful of God's peace. Physically and spiritually she was open to attack. She didn't always understand what was happening in her life but she was content to leave matters to God.

Mary's ginger hair might have suggested that she was never going to be submissive or give in to pressures. She needed to be aggressive and assertive but she needed to have these characteristics under the control of God. *'We have peace with God through our Lord Jesus Christ.' (Romans 5:1.)*

And *'For God was pleased to have all His fullness dwell in Him and through Him to reconcile to Himself all things… by making peace through His blood, shed on the cross.' (Colossians 1:20.)*

'If it is possible, as far as it depends on you, live at peace with everyone.' (Romans 12:18.)

The world thinks it can get peace through possessions, not realising that acquiring more only leads to a desire for even more. Satisfaction is never reached. Anxiety in itself is not a sin but the problems should be handed over to God; He knows what is best. Sometimes anxiety and concern are appropriate but matters still need to be in God's control.

Towards the end of her life Mary suffered many illnesses; she had never been careful of her own health. She had rheumatism which became worse during the rainy season and damp climate. This was accentuated by the fact that her houses were often built to European designs not suitable for the jungle. The best designs were the African ones. The natives had been building in the jungle for a longer time.

At one point Mary was covered from head to foot by boils. She also had an intestinal ailment. Often she had fevers brought on by being drenched by the tropical rains and remaining in her sodden clothes while she dealt with some emergency. She put the needs of others before herself. Another time she had a serious illness, the cause of which was never diagnosed. For this she had to go to the hospital at Itu where Dr Robinson nursed her.

Dr Hitchcock, a new doctor who arrived at Itu when Dr Robinson went on furlough, diagnosed that Mary wasn't having enough to eat, so he sent her a fowl to supplement her diet.

'Why have you sent me that fowl?' she asked.

'Because it wouldn't come by itself.' He obviously had a sense of humour.

So then Mary had to eat meat twice a day which she thought was an absolute unnecessary extravagance. Mary had another episode of the same illness and by the end of May she was unable to move. As cycling was now out of the question and she still needed to continue her visiting, she had a cart made which only needed two boys to pull it. A previous cart had required the use of four lads so this one was more convenient.

Early in 1911 Mary still had great plans for the future. A mission was being built at Ibiacu but the work was progressing very slowly. Mary wanted completion. In her early sixties she then moved to the new territory of Ikpe. The two-day canoe journey was very beautiful with water lilies and other colourful flowers and ferns on the water. Gambolling monkeys, butterflies and dragonflies glinted in the sunlight while snakes slid down old tree trunks and disappeared back into the jungle. It was on this journey that the canoe was attacked by a hippo. It is said that Mary had to fight it off with a pan. It seemed nothing was going to stop this indomitable lady.

All during her ministry Mary was grateful for the parcels of clothing and other items that the missions were receiving. In June 1911 it was recorded that parcels were still being received. One reason that Mary was pleased to receive these parcels from Britain was because she had a rule that she would never receive gifts from the Africans in case they connected worship of God with the paying out of money. She wanted their worship to be free and spontaneous.

The status of women in Africa was changing; to a great extent this was due to the endeavours of Mary. She always cared about the welfare of the women and even had occasion to take issue with the Biblical Paul. She wasn't always in agreement with what he said in his letters. She felt he was wrong saying wives should be in subjection to their husbands. In the margin of one of her Bibles she wrote, 'Na, na Paul laddie, this will not do.'

Chapter 12

THE WORK COMPLETED

JUST WHEN MARY was at her weakest and suffering from advanced age, disaster struck the area. In every region natives were being felled by a high fever. After four days those affected developed a nasty rash which then developed into angry pimples which broke, scabbed and left the victims badly scarred. They were the fortunate ones, for many died. The traders had brought the dreaded disease of smallpox to the region. As the people had little natural resistance against this killer disease the death rate was very high. The only answer was mass vaccination but the natives didn't trust the officials to do this. Therefore it was up to Mary to do the job, but they were suspicious of even her. Then she had an idea.

'See this mark on my arm?' she said as she rolled up the sleeve of her blouse. 'That is where I received my smallpox vaccination, which means I will never get smallpox because this is a disease which can kill you without this jab.'

'Oh, we just thought that was your fetish—we called it 'white man's juju'.'

From then on Mary was very busy vaccinating everyone she could, but even so the death toll was quite high. Mary lost some of her particular friends. One of the first victims was her close ally, Chief Ekponyong. One of the saddest times was when Edem, the chief of Ekenge caught the disease. She kept a constant watch by his bedside but was not able to save him.

Everyone else had fled so she had to bury him on her own with as much dignity as she could muster. It was a wonder she found enough strength for this task. She laid him out carefully in his best robes and top hat with his sceptre beside him.

Although the smallpox outbreak had been contained, Christmas 1911 was not a happy time for Mary. Illness seemed to be stalking her on every front. In her weakened state she contracted dysentery which meant she was unable to eat much though she was still able to enjoy a small amount of Scottish shortbread sent especially for the season.

Another of her problems was acute deafness. No longer was she able to use the gift of her tuning fork. As well as her deafness being due to old age, she knew that her ears had been damaged by the intense noise in the jute factory so many years ago. By now she had lost all her teeth, mainly due to her love of toffees which were sent from Britain on a regular basis. She never got used to her dentures.

In spite of all this Mary still managed to carry out many duties. She had now worked for well over thirty-five years on the continent which was still being described as the 'white man's grave'. She remembered hearing the stories from years ago that when missionaries and explorers went to Africa they took their coffins with them. She had the feeling that she would soon be in need of one herself.

Failing health meant she had to leave her work at Ikpe and move to Duke Town and then she was able to have the first and only holiday of her life. With Janie it was arranged that she should go to the Canary Islands. This was paid for by a generous Scotsman who remained anonymous. For one month Mary and Janie were able to stay at the Santa Catalina Hotel at Las Palma. She was greeted and treated like a heroine. The managers were Mr and Mrs Edisbury who had a lame son, Radcliffe. Mary and Radcliffe struck up a special rapport and between them they made a secret treaty. This was a secret which Radcliffe was able to keep until after Mary died.

The result of her holiday was that Mary was much improved in health and amazingly was able to continue teaching, nursing, preaching, building, painting and mixing concrete. She ran the schools in the morning and in the afternoon was visiting and nursing. Mary was seeing many prayers answered, but there were still fights to be won. She lived from day to day relying on God.

'We have no more food, except for our breakfast today, but I know we shall be fed, for God answers prayer.' In spite of her growing fame she still wished to live a frugal existence; God was providing for their needs on a daily basis.

She continued to read the Bible a lot. Hundreds of margin notes were scattered in her many Bibles.

'Why are you reading the Bible again after you've read it once?' she was asked.

'Every time I read it I'm learning more about my Lord and Master.'

Mary's adopted family were growing up rapidly and she was so proud of each one of them. She knew each one had been snatched from certain death. Hard-working, steady Annie had married an upstanding African trader, Akpan Inyang, a Christian convert and living in Itu. Mary's namesake, the 'child of wonder' who survived being abandoned for a week in the jungle as an infant, was married to a man from Lagos, a handsome Christian driver of a government motorcar. Mary encouraged her girls to marry young for their own protection as she knew her own time was running out. Maggie and Alice went to the Edgerley Memorial School in Duke Town, while Dan and Asuquo attended the Hope Waddell Institute. The success of her family was the reward for saving their lives when they had been deserted and endangered twins. By June

1913 much of Mary's workload was eased by the help of Miss Ames who was now in charge at Akpap.

Then Mary received a surprising letter. It was from the Chapter General in Charge of the Order of the Hospital of St John of Jerusalem. Even the long title scared her. The King of England was the Sovereign Head and the Duke of Connaught the Grand Prior of this order. This was a further heady connection for the humble Mary. Because of her unique service to philanthropy and sacrifice to the Government and people of Nigeria, His Most Gracious Majesty King George V had conferred on her the rank of Honorary Associate.

The formal presentation of the award of a Maltese cross was to be at the Goldie Hall in Duke Town. This was all a further nightmare for this former mill girl. She wrote back to friends in Scotland, 'I don't think there is anything different in my designation. I am Mary Mitchell Slessor, nothing more and none other than the unworthy, unprofitable but most willing servant of the King of Kings. May this be an incentive to work and be better than I have ever been in the past.'

'What shall I wear?' was the next cry. Mary's clothes were of the most basic kind. The McGregors from the college sorted through the boxes sent from Scotland to find something suitable for her to wear as she went to accept this award on behalf of the mission.

The next big event in Mary's life was of a most upsetting nature. Rumour of war had been spreading but Mary hid her fears as she didn't want to alarm the others. The First World War started on 18th August 1914. Although she was far away from the action, Mary was acutely concerned at the death rate on the battlefields. This upset caused a downturn in her health; she became desperately ill with a raging fever and in the event she was not to live long enough to see the end of hostilities.

Like the rest of the world, Africa was affected by this war. Food became dearer and there was no oil for the lamps. More and more countries were drawn into the conflict. News reached the Calabar that Belgium had been invaded by the Germans and Britain had also been dragged into the fighting. Twenty or so nations became involved, among them France, Russia, Italy and finally America.

'Will the war come to Africa?' her little ones asked.

'We must pray that it doesn't.'

Parts of Africa were indeed involved. Conflict reached the Cameroon port of Duala when British soldiers shelled the area and captured Buea, the capital of Cameroon. This was the nearest the war came to Calabar.

In one of her last letters home Mary had written, 'I can't say definitely whether I shall yet come in March, if I be spared till then.' It was not to be. She became more ill and realised she was going to die. She wasn't afraid of death itself but she had one big fear.

'I don't want to die in the bush,' she lamented. 'If I do my body parts will be used for heathen worship.'

'Your body will be safe at Use,' she was told.

To get her to Use the canoe party set out on the journey via Ikpe. As they paddled through the water-lilies, Mary's yellow cat, who had been her companion for many years, escaped and was never seen again. Maybe the animal kingdom has a sixth sense. The boys rowed sadly down the Creek and then carried Mary the three miles to Use where she was to remain.

In the mud hut with the cement floor and iron roof, Mary's final illness involved acute dysentery; she didn't have long to live. On January 10th 1915 she managed to conduct her usual service but after the meeting she became unconscious. Dr Robertson from the Mary Slessor Hospital at Itu came and revived her, but by the 12th she found it almost impossible to speak. The diarrhoea and vomiting was a lethal combination in one so weak. As she lay in much pain Martha Peacock was with her as well as members of her African family.

Once settled she lay suffering and struggling. Her family looked on heart-broken; they couldn't imagine life without her. Day and night Janie, Annie, Maggie and Alice looked on; there was so little they could do to ease her pain. Her last words were, *'O Abassi, sana mi yok*, O God release me.' On the 13th January a cock crowed at 3.30 in the morning and the assembled party mistakenly thought it was dawn as Mary breathed her last. Aged sixty-six, this worn out servant of the Lord went to her reward.

'Adiaha Makara is dead,' her family wailed. Thirty-nine of her sixty-six years had been spent in her adopted land of Africa.

Very quickly her body was carried and transported along the Cross River to Duke Town where English and Efik services were held and conducted by Rev Wilkie and Mr Rankin. As her body was ready to be buried, two very appropriate hymns were sung, 'When the day of toil is done' and 'Asleep in Jesus.' The coffin was wrapped in a Union Jack and gently lowered into the grave by teachers from Duke Town. In the grave next to hers were the bodies of William and Louise Anderson, her faithful friends who had predeceased her by a number of years. The whole of Duke Town was in mourning. Union flags flew at half-mast in memory of her life and in honour of her death. The streets were lined with troops, missionaries, schoolchildren and students from the Hope Waddell Institute, as well as hundreds of Africans. There is little to show where she was buried, just a simple cairn to mark the place. This would have pleased Mary who never wanted 'blarney and publicity.'

Messages of condolence arrived from all over the world. Her friends in Scotland were saddened and remembered her visits back home when she was accompanied by several of her children. One person described her as 'essentially energetic, resolute, businesslike, supremely courageous and not the least sentimental.'

The plot of land where Mary was buried had previously been used to bury slaves; now missionaries were buried there. Rather appropriate, really. At the head of the grave sat Mammy Fuller, Mary's native friend through all the years. As she sat there she cried out, 'Do not, do not cry. Praise God from whom all blessings flow. Ma was a great blessing.'

The Mother of the people 'Eka Kpukpro Owo' was dead. The rose which had been given to Mary when she was given the Maltese cross had rooted and was planted by the grave.

There would be no more letters to Radcliffe, who now revealed the secret he had with Mary. Daily they had both prayed that he would get better and this they had both faithfully done. Much prayer on his behalf had been answered. He now lived in Liverpool and was able to get about better on crutches for about two to three hours each day and was quite mobile with the use of a tricycle.

But Mary's fame was such that the burial plot wasn't enough. On the hillside above Duke Town there still stands an imposing memorial in the form of a huge cross gifted by the people of Scotland.

When the memorial was erected Charles Ovens commented, 'It'll tak mair than that tae holf doon oor Mary.' Mr MacGregor said, 'Mary was a whirlwind and an earthquake and a still small voice all in one. Few men or women have served God and man better than Mary Slessor.' The Governor General said, 'It is with deepest regret that I learn of the death of Miss Slessor. Her death is a great loss to Nigeria.'

Her meagre possessions were sent back to Scotland. They included a few faded garments, two Bibles, a hymn book, pebble brooch, hair bracelet, two lockets, her mother's wedding ring, watch, compass, fountain pen and the tuning fork she had been gifted. Along with these items were the two books which Charles Morrison had given her.

Mary had taken to heart the text *'Do not be overcome by evil, but overcome evil with good.' (Romans 12:21.)* Evil had been all around Mary in Calabar; with God's help she attempted to overcome this with good. Kindness and love were extended to the mothers of twins, often putting Mary's own life at risk.

Kindness was something she ceaselessly received from others. Firstly, there had been her mother who at her knee had taught her children about God. There was the Rev Logie from Wishart Church who trained her to work with the underprivileged in Dundee and then gave her a good reference when recommending her for the mission field during her period at college. The missionaries in Africa were good to Mary when she first arrived in Calabar, although at times they were scandalized at her behaviour.

Mary gained the kindness of various chiefs and to a great extent from the many twins who grew up to work with her and help her in her numerous tasks. In our goodness we are asked to look to the interests of others and consider others better than ourselves. Grace and kindness are intertwined.

'It is by grace you have been saved—through faith and this is not from yourselves; it is the gift of God.' (Ephesians 2:8.)

Chapter 13

THE WORK GOES ON

AFTER THE DEATH of any great person their lives can be judged by the work that is carried on after they have gone. What difference did they make? In the eleventh chapter of Hebrews many people are listed who 'made a difference'. Most of the verses in this chapter commence with the words 'by faith', showing that it is by faith that the difference is made. Throughout the Biblical centuries God has used faithful people to do His work and spread His word. What a stunning list it is in this chapter of Hebrews—Abel, Enoch, Noah, Abraham, Isaac, Jacob, Joseph, Moses and Rahab.

But it is not only in Biblical times that God has used such people. All during the centuries and up to the present day there have been people who have done His work, many unknown and unsung.

Mary Slessor was among that number, though not unknown or unsung. She worked faithfully for her Lord and suffered physically. Like those in Hebrews, she was jeered at, had the equivalent of stoning, went about in her versions of sheepskins and goatskins, was destitute, persecuted and ill-treated, wandered in deserts (or jungles in her case) and mountains and lived in caves and holes in the ground or at least inferior mud huts. She is to be commended for faith.

With the dynamic Mary gone the jungle claimed back some of her building work. The church which had been built by 'Ma' at Ikpe was destroyed by a falling palm tree. The house on the hilltop at Odoro Ikpe was blown down by a tornado and part of the roof carried away into the valley below. But with the arrival and control of the British, the area was opening up. Instead of having to travel along dusty tracks and wade knee-deep through swamps, many new roads were being built. This made communications easier and tribal ways more civilized.

The family were also moving on. The young girls Maggie and Alice were given a home by Martha Peacock, while young Whitie, the last girl to join the family, remained at Use near to Jean and Annie and their husbands. The first member of the family, Janie, also known as Jean, faithfully continued Mary's evangelising work until she died in the influenza outbreak in 1918. Dan was found work with the Nigerian Forestry Commission and later became a journalist. Asuquo pursued a career at sea. It was not recorded what happened to the three unmarried girls.

The work that Mary started was continued by others. Mary was the trail-blazer. Martha Peacock, Mina Amess and Beatrice remained in Calabar to continue and consolidated the work. After her husband died Agnes Young, now Agnes Arnot, returned to Calabar and became the first Mary Slessor Memorial missionary to carry on the work. The women's work moved to Arochuku and was expanded. Several outstations were established around Ikpe. As the area opened up and the work increased there were many new things to absorb and ways which Mary would have found alien to her.

Dundonians were always proud of its connection with Mary Slessor. It was in their city that she grew up, worked in one of their mills, preached in their slum areas and from there set sail to Africa. Her furloughs were mainly spent in Dundee and during her lifetime the people of the city sent out money and gift parcels to sustain her in her work.

Dundee honoured her memory, as it was on the 28th September 1923 that a magnificent window dedicated to her life was unveiled at the Museum and Art Galleries, now known as the McManus Galleries and Museum. Designs for the window were received from artists from Edinburgh, Birmingham, Glasgow and London, with the final choice finally falling on William Aikman of London. These two windows, comprising twenty pictures, depict among others, Mary at her loom and on the mission field of Africa.

The inscription reads: 'Erected by many admiring friends to the glory of God and in memory of Mary Slessor, Dundee factory girl, pioneer missionary, Old Town white Queen of Okoyong and member of the order of St John of Jerusalem, born 1848, died 1915.'

About 450 people attended the unveiling with many important dignitaries among their number. The Ex-Lord Provost Longair, Dr J.T.T. Ramsay, who had become a personal friend of Mary during her furloughs, and Mr W.P.L. Livingstone, author of *Mary Slessor in Calabar*, who as a child had helped to collect money for Mary, were both there. Naturally the many tributes paid to Mary she would have felt were unnecessary.

Extracts from the *Courier* the next day read: 'Two artistic stained glass windows in memory of Mary Slessor, the Dundee factory girl who became a distinguished African missionary were unveiled in the Albert Institute, Dundee yesterday afternoon.' This window is depicted on the cover of this book

Other parts of Britain also remembered her. In 1932 a stained glass with three lights was erected in All Saints Church, High Wycombe, Buckinghamshire, in a window which commemorated famous woman. Among the eleven women featured were Elizabeth Fry, Florence Nightingale and our Mary Slessor.

Thirty years later on the 11th September 1953 a Mary Slessor Corner was opened in the McManus Museum by the

Moderator of the Church of Scotland and an elderly Agnes Young was an honoured guest.

Although there are no working mills now within the city of Dundee, the Verdant Works Mill is a museum which depicts very much how the Baxter mill would have been in 1900. Looking at the machinery it is easy to imagine Mary working with her books propped up as she drove her loom and studied.

In 1953 Queen Elizabeth II, in her coronation year, visited the grave of Mary in Nigeria. It was her great grand-father in his role as monarch who had sanctioned Mary's membership to the order of St John of Jerusalem.

The story continues as the Mary Slessor Foundation, a Dundee-based charity is dedicated to continuing her work in the Akpap Okoyong region just fifty kilometres north of the modern Calabar. The area now has two bore holes, a medical facility, a skill centre and a palm oil/cassava processing unit. The Foundation is in partnership with the Voluntary Service Overseas (VSO) which helps to maintain the training programme. Unfortunately there is still corruption in the area.

In 1998 Mary Slessor was featured on the £10 bank notes issued in Scotland by the Clydesdale Bank. These notes are still legal tender today. Mary was the first female to be given such recognition. The obverse picture depicts Mary holding African children in her arms alongside a map of the Ekoi and Ibibio in Calabar.

Something else which would have pleased Mary very much was that her image replaced that of David Livingstone, her hero and inspiration. Livingstone appeared on the £10 notes from 1983 to 1986 and again 1993 to 1998.

When Francis Ita Udom, the great grandson of Annie, a rescued twin child of Mary saw his home village featured on the bank note, he was able to discover a great deal about his heritage. Previously he had known very little about Mary Slessor and her work.

Mary's story is not over yet as Mike Gibb, a significant Aberdeen playwright, has written and produced a musical based on her life, *Mother of All the People* which is being well received in Dundee and other Scottish cities. In 2001 the song writer Geordie McIntyre composed a song in her memory which was published in his song book, *Inveroran* and published by Lyngham House in 2005. It included the verse:

> *'A majority is God plus one' that's what Mary would aye say,*
> *It gave her courage to go on until her very dying day.*

In Aberdeen the City Council has recently unveiled a sculpture to her memory in the two and a half acre Union Terrace Gardens.

The name and work of Mary Slessor lives on. She is well-known and remembered in Scotland and although it is now a hundred years since her death, her popularity has not diminished. Indeed her life story is often used in schools under the subject of Citizenship in both England and Scotland.

Mary is a role model even today, as her God was and is able to use the humble and lowly. The only requirement of anyone is to be available to God.

The only conclusion can be words from the Bible, words which Mary would have read so often:

> *'The world and its desires pass away, but the man who does the will of God lives for ever.'*
> *(1 John 2:17.)*

Bibliography

The White Queen of Okoyong by W.P.Livingstone, Hodder and Stoughton

Mary Slessor, the Barefoot Missionary by Elizabeth Robertson. NMS Enterprises Ltd. Publishing ISBN (10) 1 901663 50 7

Servant to the Slave by Catherine Mackenzie. Christian Focus Pub. Ltd.
ISBN 078 1 85792 348 3

Mary Slessor: Faith in West Africa, Ambassador Emerald International.
ISBN 1932307 25 7

Mary Slessor, Queen of Calabar: Heroes of Faith. Barbour Publishing Inc.

Mary Slessor, J.J.Ellis, John Ritchie Ltd., Kilmarnock, Scotland

Acknowledgements, also, for help received from the McManus Archives, Dundee.

Review by Irene Howat

From Jute to Jungle:
The Mary Slessor Story

The story of Mary Slessor is one that has fired imaginations over all the generations since she went to Calabar in 1876. Carol Purves traces her history back to her roots in Aberdeen and to her childhood in Dundee. One of the writer's strong points is that from time to time throughout the story she gives snippets of information that bring the story alive. During Mary's years as a mill girl in Dundee Carol weaves in some interesting facts about the production of jute.

The book manages to capture beautifully, and rather breathlessly, the excitement, thrill, impatience and enthusiasm of Mary Slessor's early days in Calabar, an excitement, thrill, impatience and enthusiasm that never left her in all her years of missionary service there. After her death it was said of her that 'Mary was a whirlwind and an earthquake and a still small voice all in one.' The writer captures that throughout the story and leaves us in awe of this red-headed Scot, who must have left some formidable African chiefs trembling in her wake, especially if their treatment of their wives was less than respectful.

Dogged by ill-health in her later years, Mary went on with her work regardless, just adapting her mode of travel to suit her health. Her trusty bicycle had to be abandoned and eventually she was pulled round in a cart by two boys. Carol Purves cleverly conveys Mary Slessor's approach. What to some might have seemed to be giving in to increasing disability, Mary saw as the means to continue what she was able to do. And she did that to the end.

Mary Slessor is probably best remembered for saving the lives of twin babies who were abandoned in the jungle to die. But there is much more to the feisty Scot than that. Carol Purves's book will open readers' eyes to a life lived to the full for Jesus. A contemporary said, 'Few men or women have served God and man better than Mary Slessor.' I commend this story of her life.

Irene Howat